D0982723

THE DARWEN COUNTY
HISTORY SERIES

A History of
HERTFORDSHIRE

Welwyn village from Hobbs Hill

THE DARWEN COUNTY
HISTORY SERIES

A History of
HERTFORDSHIRE

Tony Rook

Phillimore

1997

Published by
PHILLIMORE & CO. LTD.
Shopwyke Manor Barn, Chichester, West Sussex

First published 1984
Second edition 1997

ISBN 1 86077 015 0

Printed and bound in Great Britain by
BUTLER AND TANNER LTD.
Frome, Somerset

Contents

List of Illustrations

Frontispiece: Welwyn village from Hobbs Hill

List of Colour Illustrations

Introduction and Acknowledgements

When I wrote the first edition of this book I had no idea of the success it would enjoy, nor of the changes it would bring to my life. The process of putting it together took me all over Hertfordshire and opened my eyes to a new way of looking at the world, and the many aspects of its history and geography. Today I travel to the same places where I am a guest speaker at clubs, societies and women's institutes and also a tutor for the Workers' Educational Association. I now teach others what I learned— and in the process I'm still learning.

As I expected, some people have asked me why I haven't paid attention to their individual interests. My answer is that, like a map, a history book can't include everything; the only full-scale map of a place is the place itself, and you can't carry that around with you! There are as many histories as there are historians, and this is only a history of Hertfordshire—mine. The reader is encouraged to produce his own.

I have received help, advice and information from many people. Librarians, curators, archivists, amateur historians, and 'Hertfordshire Hedgehogs' have patiently provided grist to my mill, and I must particularly thank the friendly and helpful staff at the County Record Office and Local Studies Library at County Hall. So many sources have been consulted that space and my inefficient memory make it impossible to acknowledge them all, and I trust that fellow authors and enthusiasts will accept here my apologies and thanks for the information which I have incorporated without acknowledgement.

I would like to thank the following for permission to reproduce photographs: The Marquess of Salisbury (colour plate VI), Hertfordshire Record Office (colour plate XI), Peter Clayton (plate 22), John Dettmar (plate 25), Clive Partridge (plate 30), Dennis Hardy (plate 158), The Board of Trinity College, Dublin (plate 59), British Aerospace (plate 172), North Herts Museum Service (plates 142, 143, 144). The rest of the artwork—the photographs, the drawings and the maps—are 'all my own work'. These, especially the photographs, could not have been produced without the assistance of my wife Merle who has taken (and still takes) me around—and others, especially Harry Bott, who have literally taken me over—the county.

Joy Trevarthen, Jack Parker and Merle read drafts of the first edition and made helpful comments; Arthur Jones critically read the first edition and kindly made suggestions for improvements. The final editing and presentation was done by the dedicated staff of Phillimore and Company. Merle proof-read this edition, as she did the first. Errors, omissions and imperfections are my own, and have been allowed despite the careful attention of so many people. My cup runneth over.

1

The Face of the County

Hertfordshire is spread over the north side of the London basin like a tattered piece of cloth, with two of its corners just overhanging the rim. In its six hundred or so square miles it contains none of the mineral deposits that excited the avarice or supplied the power of the Industrial Revolution, and there is no spectacular scenery to encourage a flourishing tourist industry. Until the county became the site of several of the artificially-created New Towns, with their imported industries, almost all its wealth came from two sources: from agriculture, and from the provision of services to travellers passing through.

Today we are almost indifferent to the landscape and to the natural factors that hitherto have guided, and even dictated, the story of the

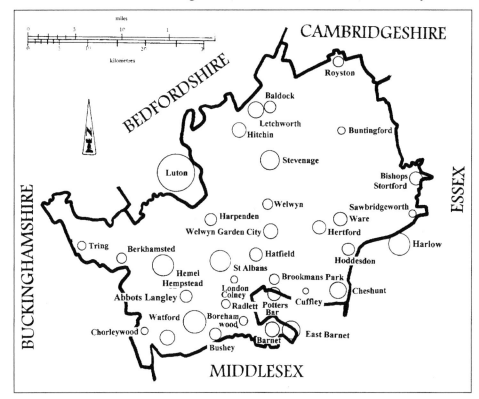

1 *This is the outline of Hertfordshire employed throughout this book, with towns indicated. It uses the boundaries of the county which were established by 1906 and maintained until the creation of the Greater London Council in 1965, when Barnet was transferred to London, and Potters Bar to Hertfordshire. Middlesex ceased to exist at this time.*

2 *Fossil from boulder clay: Gryphaea or 'devil's toe nail'*

county and its inhabitants. To speed the heedless motorist, a terrible gash has been carved from the side of Digswell Hill for the A1(M) motorway. The material from this wound has been piled across the once beautiful Mimram Valley at Lockleys. Modern engineering skills and a prodigal use of energy enable us today to create roads and settlements where there were none before, and we often ignore anything that gets in the way of these developments—even the irreplaceable traces of our past.

It must be remembered, however, that for most of its long history what events took place in the county, where people lived, how they earned their daily bread, where and by what routes they journeyed and what they saw and experienced, were all largely determined by the land itself, its hills and valleys, its soils and water supplies. Any historical survey must first try to understand the landscape and the materials from which it was made.

By geological standards, the rocks of Hertfordshire are young. Our oldest stratum still in place (there are older fragments of rock scattered about on the surface) is a hundred-million-year-old heavy blue-grey clay called *gault*. Although gault is found in only two small areas in the north and west of the county, this clay is extremely important, since it forms a layer impermeable to water (a sort of natural damp-proof course) under the entire region. Laid down in the warm sea which once covered southern Britain, it contains a wealth of marine fossils, including the beautiful glossy spiral ammonites. After the gault had been deposited, the sea became clear and clean, and there was no mud or silt to cloud the waters. Microscopic sea creatures lived in these waters, and at their death sank slowly to the bottom. For nearly thirty million years this process continued, to form a layer of white limestone over two hundred metres thick. This is the chalk of which the Chilterns are made. Since it is easily penetrated by water, it forms the best drained areas of the county.

When the chalk had been laid down, slight movements of the crust of the earth raised it for 15 million years before it sank slowly again into brackish water, at the bottom of which a 15-metre-thick layer of clays, sand and pebbles—the Reading Beds—was formed. After more earth movements, a stiff grey clay—London Clay—settled into a stratum 100 metres thick. These clays now only cover the southern area of the county between Rickmansworth and Bishop's Stortford. Other layers followed, but they have since weathered away, except for small patches of a sandy layer (the Sandgate Beds) in a few places.

3 *The solid geology of the county. The gault clay forms a continuous 'damp course' under the porous chalk.*

About thirty million years ago, by a titanic collision of the continents, the Alps were formed. On the fringes of this great event, Britain's young rocks were pushed into a series of large but gentle wrinkles, and raised again from the sea. Weather and exposure wore away the soft rocks, leaving the hard or porous rocks as hills. One wrinkle formed the geological area known as the London Basin, although its shape is more that of an old-fashioned grocer's scoop. The sides are the chalk hills, the North Downs and the Chilterns. It is closed at one end by the Berkshire Downs, and its open end faces the Channel. Right in the middle, like a dollop of cold porridge, sits the London clay, on top of which is London itself.

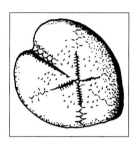

4 *Fossil from chalk — sea urchin*

One particular sequence of events exerted a great influence upon the formation of the landscape. On four occasions during the past 600,000 years, the temperature fell so low that permanent snowfields were formed in the highlands of Scandinavia and northern Britain, snowfields so thick that they became great walls of ice and swept southwards as glaciers. On two occasions they reached as far as Hertfordshire. The most recent of these occasions—about two hundred thousand years ago—has left the most obvious traces. The sheer weight of the glacier meant that it carried with it large quantities of the rocks over which it passed, and these were left behind in new locations when the ice melted. These deposits are called 'drift' and form a thin layer over most of the eastern side of the county. Much of it consisted of rock fragments and chalk; this is the chalky boulder clay which is found in the north-eastern highlands of the county. The great ice wave broke on the Chilterns, pouring over and eroding their eastern end as far west as Hitchin. This is why the hills become progressively less impressive as you travel eastwards towards Cambridge.

To add to this confused pattern, there are deposits left behind by the weathering of the rocks. As the chalk dissolves in rainwater, minute traces of clay are left. These have accumulated to give a brown deposit which contains frost-shattered flints, and pebbles from the Reading Beds. This 'clay-with-flints' survives in the west of the county, where the glaciers did not reach. All kinds of weathering affect the picture. The rock deposits are broken up by freezing and thawing, wetting and drying, penetration by roots and burrowing animals. Fine particles tend to be washed down by percolating water and worked upwards by worms. Rain is slightly acidic, and other acids are produced by the decomposition of dead plants and animals. These acids tend to dissolve slightly alkaline soils like chalk and limestone.

5 *Diagram of the ice flow over the county in the Anglian Ice Age. Lake St Albans is formed where the proto-Thames has been dammed.*

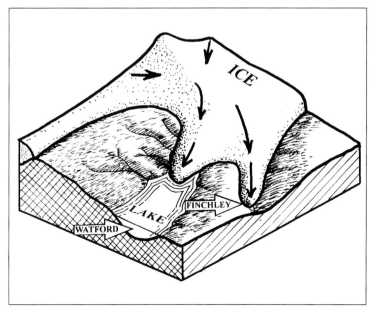

Acidic soils are relatively infertile; but fortunately most soils in Hertfordshire were initially rich in chalk, and the importance of

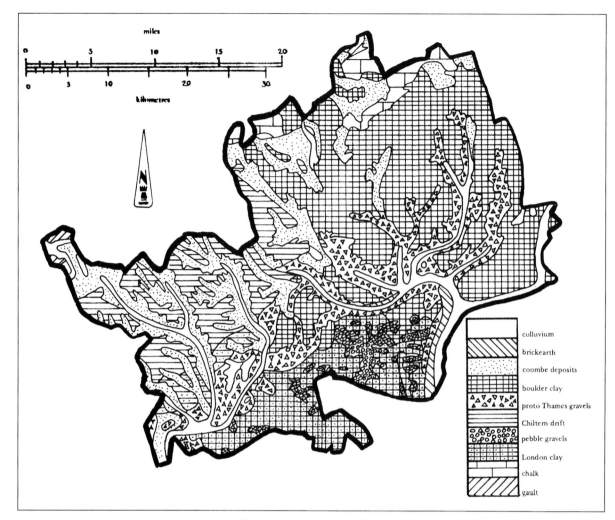

miles

kilometres

	colluvium
	brickearth
	coombe deposits
	boulder clay
	proto Thames gravels
	Chiltern drift
	pebble gravels
	London clay
	chalk
	gault

6 *'The soils of the county mix and run into each other in a remarkable manner.' A simplified soils map of Hertfordshire.*

7 *Chalkdrawers*

preventing acidity has been appreciated since early times, probably since the Iron Age. Chalk has been dug for many centuries to add to acid soils and render them more alkaline. A notable feature of the Hertfordshire landscape is the large number of now derelict chalk pits, which appear either as tree-filled or ploughed-out depressions, usually on the shoulders of valleys where the chalk outcrops. On plateaux, and elsewhere where the quarrying of chalk was seen as an uneconomical use of land, it was common, up to the early years of this century, to mine it on the spot. D. Walker, in his *General Views of the Agriculture of the County of Hertfordshire*, wrote in 1795:

> The pit is sunk 20 to 30 feet deep, and then chambered at the bottom, that is, the pitman digs or cuts out the chalk horizontally, in three separate directions; the horizontal apertures being of a sufficient height and width to admit the pitman's working in them with ease and safety. One pit will chalk six acres, laying sixty loads on an acre.

Since the quoted 60 loads per acre amounts to 45 tons, each pit would yield about 270 tons, leaving a space about 220 cubic yards in volume—the size of a small house! It is not surprising, therefore, that from time to time 'swallow holes' appear in fields, and that this can lead to unfortunate consequences for new housing estates—for instance, the 'Panshanger' estates in Welwyn Garden City.

The bewilderingly complex pattern of the drift geology of the county has thus combined with subsequent natural erosion and human activities to give a soil pattern of great complexity, where a number of soil types may be found in the same fields. The agricultural writer Arthur Young warned in 1804 of the consequences of this for anyone attempting to map the county's geology:

> The truth is, that the soils of this county mix and run into each other in a remarkable manner; so that, except in the case of chalk, and that singularly infertile land which I have termed gravel, they are traced and named with a good deal of uncertainty.

The texture of the soil—whether light, gravelly, or heavy clay—has to a large extent determined the chronological order of use. As the

8 *Fossil from gault ammonite*

9 *Soil drainage and acidity in the county. This map should be compared with the distribution of Roman and Domesday settlements.*

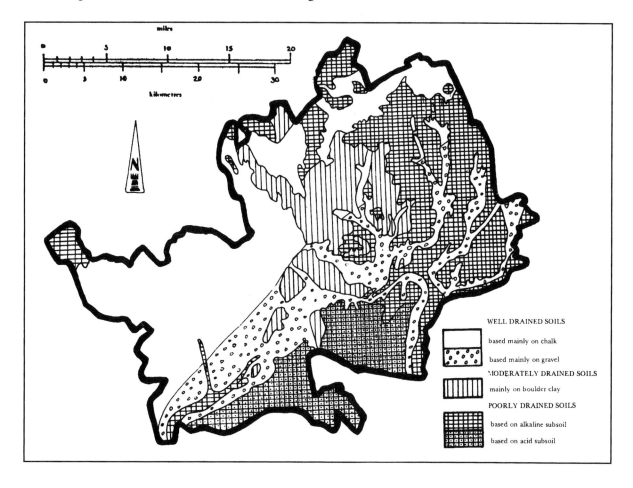

WELL DRAINED SOILS

based mainly on chalk

based mainly on gravel

MODERATELY DRAINED SOILS

mainly on boulder clay

POORLY DRAINED SOILS

based on alkaline subsoil

based on acid subsoil

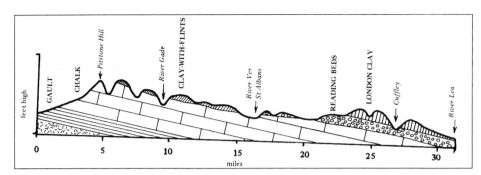

10 *Diagrammatic section across the county. The vertical scale is greatly exaggerated.*

plough and other more advanced farming implements were developed, so agriculture spread to less easily-worked soils. Drainage may often prove critical, since a waterlogged soil in springtime can cause a disastrous failure in germination; most of the 'lost' (i.e., abandoned) villages of Hertfordshire lay on soils described as 'poorly drained'. The light, well-drained, calcareous soils of the Chilterns have been cultivated since farming first began. The gravels of the Vale of St Albans seem to have come into use in the Belgic Iron Age. Occupation of the heavy and poorly-drained boulder clay of the north-east highlands seems to have been intense in the early medieval period; but the London Clay and Reading Beds in the south-east—not only heavy and poorly-drained but also lacking in chalk—have daunted cultivators, and so have been left to

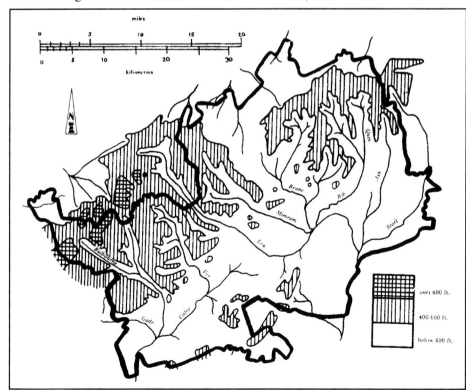

11 *Relief and rivers in Hertfordshire. Note how the Lea is captured by the proto-Thames valley and flows north-east from Hatfield. The Ver flows south-west for the same reason.*

support oak and hornbeam forest and pastureland.

The water table—the natural level of saturation in the chalk—sometimes reaches the surface, as for example at Ashwell, where the water, overflowing the gault clay at the edge of the London Basin, gives rise to the source of the Cam (locally called the Rhee). All along the scarp slope of the Chilterns is a row of villages which have grown up along the spring line where the gault outcrops. Since most of the county's rivers flow on chalk, often because they cut their valleys through any superficial deposits, it is clear that the river levels must coincide with the water tables in

12 *Varves at Mill Green, Hatfield. These are thin layers of fine mud laid down annually at the bottom of 'Lake St Albans' as the glacier retreated at the end of the Anglian Ice Age (see plate 5).*

the valleys. Some rivers and streams flow only when the water table is abnormally high after heavy rain, and are called 'bournes'. The resurgence of a bourne is often thought to foretell disaster, and another name for them is 'woe waters'. It may be significant that many bournes rise in the north-east of the county, in an area which contains many deserted medieval villages. The most noticeable thing about the river pattern of the county as a whole, seen best from a map, is the diversion of their course along a line from Rickmansworth to Ware. This can be noticed, for instance, by tracing the line of the Lea from its source high in the Chilterns. At first the river flows quite logically down the slope of the hills towards the Thames. However, when it reaches Mill Green, Hatfield, it seems to lose interest, turning sharply north-east. It is not until Ware that it seems to remember its purpose, turn south again, and make for the Thames below London. The Colne and its tributaries repeat the same sort of pattern, but the diversion here is south-west, and they reach the Thames upstream of London. The explanation of this odd behaviour lies in events already described. During the Ice Age, the ice sheet that pushed over the chalk hills of East Anglia poured into what is now the Vale of St Albans, but which was at that time the valley of a much larger Thames. Lakes were formed at Wheathampstead and St Albans. Eventually the Thames cut itself a new valley further south and, when the ice retreated, the earlier valley was left for the midget rivers of Lea and Colne.

The river diversion was of lasting importance for the county, since the old Thames valley is full of rich deposits of gravel. The gravel soils proved attractive to the first Belgic settlers (see Chapter 3) and the subsoil is of great commercial importance today. Most of the principal towns of modern Hertfordshire are on this gravel.

2

Prehistory

13 *Palaeolithic 'hand axe' from Hitchin*

14 *A Mesolithic flint axe from Bishop's Stortford*

The first people to arrive in Hertfordshire were small groups of nomadic hunters and gatherers. They were few in number, and lived on what they could find during the warmer periods of the Ice Age. The period since they lived is so vast that what little traces they left have been rendered fragmentary and difficult to decipher. So far no skeletons have been found, and no remains of anything they may have made of such materials as wood, skin or bone. Luckily for archaeologists, however, from the earliest times use was made of brittle stone—especially of flint—to provide sharp cutting edges, and flint is strong enough to withstand freezing, thawing, and being tumbled along with other stones in the torrential meltwaters of the glaciers.

The oldest and most prolific of the major sites of the Palaeolithic or Old Stone Age period in the county is a gravel pit at Hill End, Rickmansworth. It has produced hundreds of flint tools. They were made by chipping off flakes of flint, and it is thought that they were probably used by hunters who lived along the proto-Thames valley (see the previous chapter) something like 350,000 years ago. Higher up in the same pit, and also at another site nearby at Croxley Green, tools known as 'ovate axes' have been found. These were made by a more advanced technique. Surviving sites where Palaeolithic people camped are very rare. The examples found in the north-east of Hertfordshire, where the glacial ice failed to reach, are therefore of national importance. Areas of the Pleistocene land surface have survived, buried under a wind-blown deposit known as 'brick earth'. This material was used for making bricks in the 19th century, and provided collectors with many fine specimens of the type of flint tool called 'hand axes'. These were probably all-purpose tools, held in the hand; they have no cutting edge like a true axe, and were either round-ended or pointed. In 1916 at Markyate Street and Gaddesden Row, the collector W.G. Smith reported finding flint working floors preserved where 'every artificial chip of flint was as sharp as a knife, and where every flint rests in the precise place where it originally fell from the hands and stone hammers of the primaeval workers in flint'. Unfortunately, in Smith's day little attention was paid to the evidence that modern archaeologists would seek in order to discover the environmental conditions that had prevailed when the flint-workers were busy, although it seems clear that this particular site was that of a camp beside a lake.

20

It seems that none of the Hertfordshire finds belong to the sophisticated cultures of the late Palaeolithic, which appear elsewhere about one hundred thousand years ago, and the next period represented by important discoveries in the county is the Mesolithic or Middle Stone Age. Following the last retreat of the ice, Britain had become an island. The climate had become warm and damp, and the country was covered by forests. The river valleys, which by this time followed the same courses as today, provided plentiful game for the hunters who made their way into the area about 6000 B.C.

Under peat deposits in the river valleys, notably at Broxbourne, Stanstead Abbots and Cuffley, but also elsewhere, flint tools have been found which include scrapers and true axes, designed to be hafted, and presumably intended for use in tree-cutting. From finds elsewhere in Britain, it is known that the Mesolithic hunters felled trees to make riverside platforms, and hunted pigs and deer. They also snared wildfowl and caught fish. On some sites large numbers of very small flint barbs are found, intended as arrowheads. A bone harpoon was found at Fowlmere, Royston.

Although the Mesolithic hunters made artificial clearings in the forests, it was not until the Neolithic or New Stone Age (about 3500 B.C.) that man's impact upon the landscape became really significant,

15 *The Neolithic long barrow on Therfield Heath is known to have contained one burial. The accompanying round barrows may be Neolithic or Bronze-Age. The other earthworks are part of a modern golf course.*

16 *A Neolithic axe from Ware*

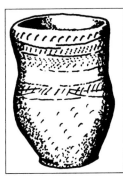

17 *Beaker from Tewin*

with the arrival of real farming. Since primitive agriculture could only cope with light soils, this period sees the start of the domination of the county's settlement pattern by the chalk ridge of the Chilterns, which was to continue until the Belgic invasions of the first century B.C., and the establishment of communications along the Icknield Belt. Two long barrows are known in Hertfordshire which represent the most easterly examples of this form of Early Neolithic burial mound. Unfortunately one of them—at Knocking Knoll, Pegsdon—was badly excavated and destroyed in 1856, and there is no record of what it contained. The long barrow on Therfield Heath is known to have contained one burial, under a pile of turves which represented what in examples further to the west would have been a burial chamber made of stones. Neolithic barrows often seem to have been used as charnel houses; one round barrow on Royston Heath contained nine disarticulated skeletons.

A site of the type known as a 'causewayed camp', surrounded by a discontinuous ditch, has been found at Rickmansworth. Such places were probably used as meeting places, perhaps not unlike medieval fairgrounds. Late Neolithic pottery has been found at several sites in the county, such as Codicote Heath and Pishiobury, as well as in five funnel-shaped pits found near Blackhorse Road, Letchworth. These pits also contained the bones of wild animals, such as deer and hares, as well as those of domesticated animals like cattle and dogs.

The Neolithic farmers used hafted axes made of polished stone. The distribution of finds of this kind along the river valleys seems to confirm that the areas of lighter gravel were used quite extensively. Seventy specimens in museums include examples made of rocks from the highland zone of Britain and even Ireland, as well as local flint.

During the latter half of the second millennium B.C., the use of bronze became well established for weapons and fine tools, although flint continued in use for everyday disposable items such as knives and arrowheads. Several Bronze-Age round barrows survive, particularly along the Icknield Way. Few, however, contained contemporary pottery; in fact, it is well known that while Bronze-Age burials are widely distributed, domestic finds are rare. However, finds of this period are widely distributed. Thirteen hoards of tools, weapons and other metal objects have been discovered in Hertfordshire, apparently dating from the seventh or eighth centuries B.C. They may have been goods hidden in time of trouble, or else offerings to the gods; however, the presence of scrap metal in many hoards would seem to suggest that they were often the stock-in-trade of itinerant smith-merchants.

Iron-using people arrived in Hertfordshire about 600 B.C., and the sites at Ravensburgh (Hexton) and Willbury (Letchworth) were occupied at this time. They developed into heavily defended 'hill-forts' with massive ditches and timber-laced ramparts, dominating the Chiltern ridge. An impressive defended site at Arbury Banks, Ashwell, and an undefended farmstead at Barley were occupied in the third century B.C. 'Forts' at The Aubreys (Redbourn), Wallbury (Little Hallingbury) and

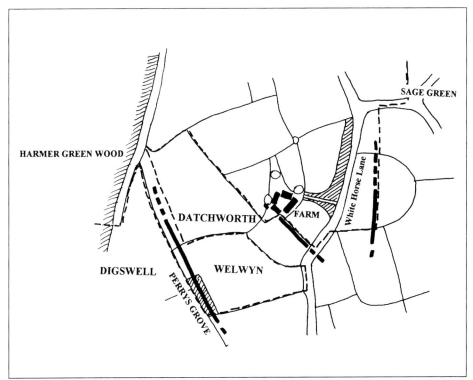

18 *Boundaries at Welch's Farm. The fine lines show the field boundaries in the nineteenth century, the dashed line the parish boundaries, and the heavy line the known and deduced course of the main Iron-Age ditches. The parish bounds follow the Iron-Age ditches where these are invisible, even in the absence of field hedges.*

Spellbrook (both just in Essex) probably represent the centres of Early-Iron-Age tribes which had penetrated into the gravel areas. At Royston an erratic and feeble triple dyke system—the Mile Ditches—which runs down the scarp slope of the Chilterns, has been suggested as a boundary or territorial marker.

The picture which emerges is of intense occupation of the open chalklands, and of penetration down the river valleys into the heavily forested hinterland to the south. The mixed gravels of the proto-Thames valley were not exploited on any scale until the arrival of the Belgae, a generation before Julius Caesar reached Britain.

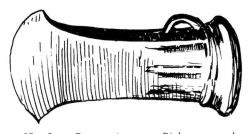

19 *Late Bronze-Age axe, Rickmansworth*

3

Belgae and Romans

20 *Coin of Tasciovanus*

21 *An impressive ditch, part of which is still visible today at Devil's Dyke. The material dug from the ditch was piled on both sides of it, to form a barrier 100 feet across from crest to crest, and 30 feet deep.*

In the first century B.C. a new group of settlers arrived in Hertfordshire. They are called 'Belgic' or 'the Belgae' because Caesar later wrote that they came from Belgium. Much later, the tribe was referred to as the Catuvellauni. They came up the Lea Valley, and made their first major settlement at Wheathampstead, where they constructed what Caesar called an *oppidum*, a fortified enclosure some hundred acres in extent, overlooking the Lea, and surrounded by an impressive ditch, part of which is still visible today at the 'Devil's Dyke'. The material dug from the ditch was piled on both sides of it, to form a barrier 100 feet from crest to crest, and 30 feet deep.

From Wheathampstead an earthwork of similar scale was dug across the plateau between the Lea and the Ver, a distance of about four miles. Part of this is also still visible as 'Beech Bottom Dyke'. As the land to the south of this earthwork would have been covered by uninhabited forest, it seems that its purpose was to provide a frontier facing north, separating land which was already occupied from virgin territory which the Belgae intended to occupy.

It is likely (though not certain) that Julius Caesar's final confrontation with Cassivellaunus, the ruler of the Catuvellauni, in 54 B.C. was at Wheathampstead. The terms which Caesar claims to have extracted from the Britons included an agreement that they would not try to expand their territory, but it is clear that they were confident enough to ignore this. By the first decade A.D. they had conquered most of south-east Britain, and had their capital city at *Camulodunum* (Colchester). *Oppida* had been constructed or taken over from their original owners. One important major settlement was at *Verulamium* (near present-day

St Albans), where coins were minted by the leader Tasciovanus with variations on the inscription VERLAMIO. Another important centre was Puckeridge. Large numbers of coins from many Belgic mints suggest a busy market here.

Numerous Belgic farms were built, many of them on the gravel plateaux which were available for the first time for agriculture thanks to the heavy 'coulter' plough which could cultivate these areas. Discoveries made during the building of Welwyn Garden City suggest that there may have been one farm about every square kilometre. The farms were surrounded by ditches with palisades, enclosing about one or two acres. Few traces apart from the rubbish in the ditches have survived, but the farmers' refuse gives us an idea of their way of life: fine wheel-thrown pottery, great storage jars for grain, triangular loom-weights and spindle whorls, along with the bones of cows, pigs, sheep, goats and horses, all attest to their economy.

The Roman writer Strabo in the early first century A.D. listed the exports Rome took from Britain: corn, cattle, gold, silver, iron, hides, slaves and clever hunting dogs. Archaeology gives us an idea what Britain imported in return: luxury goods, such as wine, silverware, furniture, fine pottery, ivory, glass and jewellery. The great *amphorae*, tall two-handled Mediterranean wine jars, are a common feature of the most spectacular remains of the late Belgic period. These are the graves known as 'Welwyn-type Chieftain Burials', after the area where several of them have been discovered. The most recently discovered example from Welwyn Garden City contained five Roman amphorae, 36 pottery vessels of various forms, a silver drinking cup of Neapolitan craftsmanship, two bronze vessels, and traces of wooden furniture with bronze fittings. There was also a gaming board with 24 coloured glass pieces. Some of this chief's followers had their cremated ashes set into the ground in pots near his grave, so as not to be separated from him after death.

22 *Grave of a Belgic chieftain from Welwyn Garden City discovered by the author and now reconstructed in the British Museum. A silver Neapolitan cup can be seen (bottom centre) and glass gaming counters (left). The imported amphorae (wine jars) are common to such burials.*

23 *Head of a Belgic Iron-Age 'firedog' from Baldock*

The Belgae were mainly farmers. They had a highly developed social organisation which may have been not unlike the later Scottish clan system, with minor chieftains and their followers owing allegiance to major chiefs whom the Romans graced with the title of 'king'. The lowest social ranking was that of slave.

Roman authority became established in Britain by gradual stages following the invasion of the Emperor Claudius in A.D. 43. Claudius chose a moment when the 'king' of the Catuvellauni, Cunobelinus or Cymbeline—who was also the chief commander of the forces of the Belgic tribes—had just died, and his territory had been divided between two of his sons, Caractacus and Cogidubnus. The Roman legions defeated the forces of these two rulers, and pressed on to establish a frontier along the line of what was later to become the Fosse Way. There was no significant battle in Hertfordshire, and no major military occupation seems to have been thought necessary.

A small detachment of soldiers stayed at *Verulamium* for a short while, to mark out the lines of a new city, intended to occupy 120 acres. This city grew and flourished, providing the Romans with a market and a centre of administration, but above all with an example of civilised living to set before the Britons. Its influence spread into the countryside

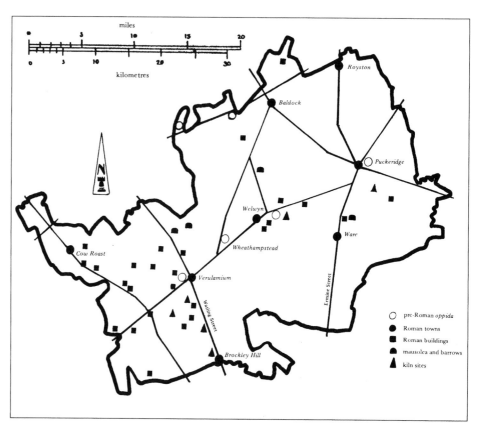

24 *Roman sites and roads in Hertfordshire. Note how most of the sites are located on the well drained soils*

too: the Romans did not replace the Britons, they transmuted them into Romans. In A.D. 60 a rebellion against Rome swept out of East Anglia, under the leadership of the Queen of the Iceni, Boudicca (Boadicea). The rebels destroyed London, Colchester and *Verulamium*. Tacitus, the Roman historian, calls the latter a *municipium* in his account of the revolt, which implies that it was a special city the inhabitants of which enjoyed Roman citizenship. Tacitus also implies that the city was undefended; there was, we know, a ditch and bank marking the boundary, but there was no wall, and apparently no garrison. It is interesting that only 17 years after the Catuvellauni had been the princi-

25 *Welwyn Baths during excavation. This site was preserved by the author in a steel vault under the A1(M) motorway, and is open to the public.*

pal opponents of the Romans, a city existed in their territory which was afforded the highest status, but which was not considered to need defending. One possible explanation is that it was built for Adminius, the third son of Cunobelinus, who had been exiled from Britain before his father's death for his pro-Roman sympathies.

Ten years after the Boudiccan rebellion, monumental public works were undertaken at *Verulamium*. A great *forum* was built, with a *curia* or council chamber and a *basilica* or town hall along one side, which was 420 feet long. Some sense of the scale of this work, and of the impression it must have made on the Britons, can be obtained by comparing it with the Norman abbey which was built nearby 1,000 years later. The basilica was the same length as the abbey, but (if we ignore the transepts) more than twice as wide.

26 *Belgic iron stand with imported Roman amphora, Welwyn*

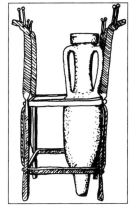

Private development in the city was still, as it had been before the rebellion, primarily of small timber-framed wattle-and-daub buildings, although the inhabitants enjoyed fine possessions, both locally produced and imported. During this period construction seems to have begun of country houses of similar design. These *villas* were often sited on or near the Belgic farmsteads which they replaced. Most of them continued to be the centre of farming estates, and their inhabitants were probably mostly Britons. As they became more sophisticated and Roman in their tastes, the villas were improved and became more luxurious.

By the middle of the second century, *Verulamium* was a bustling city which was growing out of its original boundaries. The ditch which had been dug to mark the original site was filled in, and the street pattern continued over it. In 155 there was a great fire, but rebuilding was swift. The new city was much improved, with shops and houses constructed of flint masonry, some having mosaic floors. New temples and a theatre were built. Many of the countryside villas were remodelled and improved as well at about this time.

Towards the end of the century the building impetus declined. Perhaps because of the unsettled political situation produced by the attempt of the governor of Britain, Clodius Albinus, to become emperor, an ambitious programme of defence works was undertaken around *Verulamium*. A massive rampart and ditch was intended to enclose an area nearly twice as large as the original city. Splendid masonry gateways were built at the main entrances to the city on Watling Street. The

27 *'In the early third century walls ... were constructed.' A continuous excavated length of the walls of Verulamium from the south corner, looking north-east.*

work was not completed, however, although in the early third century walls following a smaller circuit were constructed. The period from about 270 to 295 was one of political and economic instability in the Western Roman Empire. In some places the archaeological evidence is of decay; in others there was investment, perhaps by immigrants from Gaul. Some excavations in *Verulamium* have shown a gloomy picture at this time, and others have shown one of hope. Most of the villas show signs of dilapidation and even of demolition.

The obvious prehistoric routes in the county are notable for their continuity. They result from relief and geology, and were probably used even before there were any settlements. They are the Icknield Way, along the scarp slope of the Chilterns, and the routes which follow the river valleys. The only people prior to relatively recent times actually to construct roads were the Roman engineers. Their system was based on a pattern radiating from the Thames crossing-place, which became *Londinium*. The main roads of the system in Hertfordshire went through the Tring Gap (Akeman Street), through *Verulamium*

(Watling Street), and up the Lea Valley (Ermine Street). Other roads connected the towns to each other. *Verulamium* was joined to Silchester and also to Puckeridge—and so to Colchester—via Welwyn and a number of other Belgic sites, which indicates that this Roman route followed a prehistoric trackway. Puckeridge, in fact, became a nexus of roads; Stane Street, the road from Colchester, went through it and on to Sandy, joining the Icknield Way at Baldock, another Roman site. Baldock was connected via Welwyn and Wheathampstead to *Verulamium*. Many other Roman routes have been suggested, but not definitely identified.

The first half of the fourth century was a time of at least moderate prosperity, before the final slow decline. There was some rebuilding both in town and country. Most villas seem to have continued in use until the later part of the century, but there seems to have been a decline in standards, as repairs were bodged, fires lit on pavements, and industrial and agricultural processes brought into former living quarters. It may be that the owners of the villas preferred the comparative security of the towns, and left their farms to be run in their absence. At the end of the fourth century the walls of Verulamium were strengthened by the addition of bastions, which would support artillery weapons such as catapults. In 410 the Emperor Honorius responded to appeals for help from Britain, which was now under threat from Saxons and other raiding barbarian groups, by telling the Britons to look to their own defence. After nearly 400 years of Roman rule, the province of Britain was abandoned to its fate.

28 *Roman cremation burial from Puckeridge*

4

Saxon and Norman Hertfordshire

Many histories tell us that the year 410 marked the 'end of the Roman occupation of Britain' or give it as the date when the legions were withdrawn. Neither of these statements is true. In the first place every freeborn inhabitant of Britain was by birth and education a Roman citizen, as his ancestors had been for ten generations before him. Nor did the soldiers suddenly migrate; the army based in Britain had for years been gradually depleted by redeployment to the Continent. What really happened in 410 was that Honorius authorised the Britons to raise their own army and provide their own leadership.

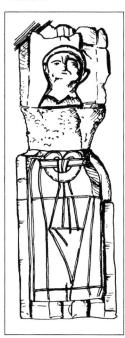

29 *Saxon figure of Christ carved in stone, Walkern*

Despite the long association of Roman civilisation with Britain, it seems, surprisingly, that from the early fifth century onwards there was a comparatively rapid abandonment of many of the refinements associated with the Roman way of life. Technologies and industries were forgotten, and in a relatively short time we find no trace of either the Celtic or the Latin tongue. Roofs lacked tiles, windows no longer had glass and the standard of pottery-making declined. With the breakdown of Roman administration, the Roman road system as a whole became neglected. Parts of it continued to be used, however, though not properly maintained, and the prehistoric trackways were also still in use. The road from *Verulamium* to Silchester disappeared, and the cross-country route to Puckeridge became broken in places. Ermine Street went out of use south of Ware, and the old valley road came back into its own.

It would be easy to explain these changes if we could say that one people replaced another; the simplistic idea that the Romans went home and the Saxons took over is, however, incorrect. Town life went on in *Verulamium*, for instance, and what evidence we have suggests that, apart from mercenaries fighting on the side of the Roman Britons, no Saxons came near the city for nearly 200 years. Very little early Saxon material has been found in Hertfordshire, but its distribution, supported by a few pagan Saxon place-names, suggests that a few isolated groups settled along the Icknield Way and in the east, between A.D. 430 and 500. The absence of Saxon settlement elsewhere in the county has led some historians to suggest that the Roman Britons based on *Verulamium* excluded the new arrivals, and established a Celtic enclave. However, this theory is as yet unsupported by any archaeological finds of the period from the area in question. The notion of a district being occupied

by a Romano-Celtic people, strong
enough and sufficiently well-organ-
ised to repel an invasion, yet using
nothing that might survive the passage of time, is not really convinc-
ing. Within a generation they
would have been obliged to abandon the way of life that had been
usual for hundreds of years, es-
chewing the use of pottery, bronze
and iron.

Nevertheless, it remains true
that the initial incursions of the
Saxons into the northern and eastern fringes of the county do not
seem to have been followed by
expansion into the areas which the
Romans had found so attractive;
on the available evidence, there
may even have been a temporary

withdrawal. No finds from most of the sixth century have been made; but
Saxon objects and even settlements dating from the end of the century
and the following one appear all over the county. One possible conclusion is that the Saxon invaders suffered a setback. About A.D. 500
(there is no definite agreement on the date) the British leader Arthur
defeated the Saxons at a great battle, known as the battle or siege of
'Mount Badon'. However, the Saxons eventually made a comeback, with
a victory at 'Bidcanford' which gave them control over an area including
Aylesbury and Luton. This happened in 571, and expansion to
Verulamium may have taken place soon afterwards.

30 *The remains of a
Saxon sunken hut
(grubenhaus) at Fox-
holes, near Hertford,
during excavation. The
archaeological evidence
for the Saxon period in
the county is slight.*

Just over a hundred years later, in 689, the first Danes arrived on
the shores of Britain. They came first as coastal raiders, and then began
to spend the winter here. Soon they had settled in the east, and raided
far inland. In 869 Edmund, last of the Anglian kings, was killed in battle,
and in 873 Burgred, successor to Offa the last ruler of the Midlands
kingdom of Mercia fled to the Continent. Hertfordshire, we may suppose, was overrun, and only Wessex in the south withstood the heathen
host. In 878 Alfred, King of Wessex, defeated the Danes, but the Saxons
(or English, as we may now call them) were not strong enough to expel
them altogether from Britain. A frontier was drawn between the Danes
and the English, which was more clearly defined after a Danish revolt in
885. The frontier ran along the River Lea in part, thus dividing the
present county of Hertfordshire in two.

31 *Blocked Saxon
doorway at Reed church*

The peace was not kept, however, and, augmented by further forces
from overseas, the Danes tried to conquer the whole country in 892.
Many battles were fought, including a victory for Alfred's son Edward
on an island in the Colne in Hertfordshire. In 895 the Danes drew their

32 *The sufferings of the English: from Matthew Paris*

ships up the Lea, and built a fort '20 miles above the city of London'. This could, perhaps, be at Hertford. Alfred camped nearby, and the *Anglo-Saxon Chronicle* records that:

> One day the king rode up along the river and looked to see here the river could be blocked so that they [the Danes] would not be able to bring out their ships. This they [the English] proceeded to do: they made two forts on the two sides of the river, but when they had just begun that operation, and had encamped thereby, the host saw that they could not bring out their ships. Thereupon they abandoned them, and went across country.

There is a strong tradition that in order to block the river, Alfred did not just rely on the forts, but undertook engineering works. Suggestions have included the construction of a weir at Ware, from which the town gets its name; braiding the river into a number of smaller streams at Cheshunt (King's Weir); or the construction of a weir at the confluence of the Lea and the Thames, called Blackwall!

The Chronicle tells us that 'the following summer ... the host dispersed, some to East Anglia, and those without stock got themselves ships and sailed overseas'. Alfred had won, and in 913 his son Edward set about the reconquest of the Danelaw:

33 *'Hertford guarded the confluence of the other river valleys with the Lea.' Aerial view of the castle from the north. The original motte is at the top of the picture, to the left of the modern pyramidal roof. The curtain wall was completed by Henry II in 1173. The brick gate-house (centre) was built between 1461-5, and its gothic windows were inserted when a new south-east wing was built in 1792.*

> In this year, after Martinmas, King Edward had the more northerly fort at Hertford built between the Maran, the Beane and the Lea. Then afterwards ... King Edward went with part of his forces to Maldon, in Essex ... and a good number of people who had formerly been under Danish domination submitted to him. Another part of his forces built a fortress at Hertford on the southern bank of the Lea.

This is the first historic mention of Hertford. The county itself must have come into being around this time, for in 1011 we find the following entry, when the Danes were pressing the English to agree to their sovereignty over a given area:

> In this year the King and his councillors sent to the host and craved peace, promising them tribute and provisions on condition that they should cease their harrying. They [the Danes] had at this time overrun (i) East Anglia, (ii) Essex, (iii) Middlesex, (iv) Oxfordshire, (v) Cambridgeshire, (vi) *Hertfordshire* ... .

It seems that the Lea formed the legal division between the English territory and that in which Danish customs prevailed (the Danelaw) for at least a generation. It was a convenient frontier, but an arbitrary one, and there is no doubt that, both before and after the treaty that established it, there were many Danish settlers on the south-west side of the river. In fact, the most westerly of the administrative districts of the

I *'One of the smallest failed villages, Caldecote, was only 325 acres in extent'. The site today with church and farm.*

II *At Datchworth the main settlement is today on the main road, having deserted the original centre of the parish round the church a mile to the north.*

III *Watton at Stone Church shows a typical example of a village which migrated to the main road. There were cottages and a village green here at the beginning of the 20th century.*

IV *Welwyn village from the south. The historic core of the village owes its existence to the flourishing coaching trade in the 18th and 19th centuries.*

county in the 10th century was the Hundred of *Danais*, meaning 'the Danes', later Latinised to *Danicorum* and later still shortened to 'Dacorum'. Throughout history the two sides of the county have shown marked differences. Many factors have inter-acted to produce their special characters, and over the length of time involved it is impossible to say how much this feature of the county is due to the occupation of the Danes.

The Danes, we are told, were successful farmers, freemen on their own holdings. When the Normans came to England in the 11th century, there were numerous small settlements in the north-east of Hertfordshire, and many freemen. The date and origin of the many moated homestead sites which occur in the north-east are uncertain; they would be ideal dwellings for independent yeomen. The pattern of settlement, and much of the character of rural Hertfordshire, however, was certainly determined by the time the Normans came.

After defeating King Harold at the Battle of Hastings, William of Normandy did not risk laying siege to the heavily defended city of London, but made his way round it, laying waste the countryside. The monkish chronicler Florence of Worcester tells us that: 'He devastated Hertfordshire, and did not stay his hand from burning the towns to ashes, or from slaughtering the people, until he came to the town called Berkhamsted'.

At Berkhamsted William was met by Prince Edgar (whom the English had elected king in succession to Harold), Archbishop Aeldred, Earl Edwin, Earl Morcar and 'all the best people from London, who submitted from force of circumstances'. We are told the surrender took place in a royal hall from which the city of London could be seen. This description and other evidence point to *Little* Berkhamsted, east of Hatfield, which was a royal estate. The Anglo-Saxon Chronicle records that after the Archbishop had crowned William king at Westminster, 'Bishop Odo [William's half brother] and Earl William ... built castles far and wide throughout the land, oppressing the unhappy people'.

Two main castles dominated Hertfordshire, about twenty miles north of the capital. Great Berkhamsted (on the west side of the county) guarded the Tring gap through the Chilterns on Akeman Street, the main road originally built by the Romans. Hertford guarded the confluence of the other river valleys with the Lea, as well as Ermine Street. A third castle, 'Waytemore', at Bishop's Stortford lay on the causeway of Stane Street across the Stort

34 *Hertford Castle in 1610 from Speed's map*

35 *'Great Berkhamsted (on the west side of the county) guarded by the Tring Gap through the Chilterns on Akeman Street.' Aerial view from the west. Because of its strategic position the castle sits beside the London and North Western Railway and the Grand Union Canal, as well as the old main road.*

36 'A great mound, or motte which was enclosed by its own ditch.' An aerial view of the tree covered motte of Anstey Castle (centre) from the south west.

37 Plan of Anstey Castle

marshes. These castles were of the commonest Norman type, the motte and bailey. The bailey was a courtyard containing the hall and domestic buildings, stables and workshops, fortified by a surrounding ditch, with the earth upcast into a bank inside, and a palisade on top. Overlooking the bailey and the surrounding countryside, and serving as a last point of defence, was a watchtower, built on top of, and sometimes partly within, a great mound, the motte, which was enclosed in its own ditch.

William's domination of England had as its fundamental philosophy the belief that all the land belonged to the Crown. Strong men held estates (fiefs) from the king, and these feudal landlords gave him homage, taxes and military service in return. They also secured the countryside against a native uprising. Most of them were Normans, rewarded with lands for their services to the Conqueror, and they had to be men of iron, for purposes of taxation, as well as to settle disputes over ownership:

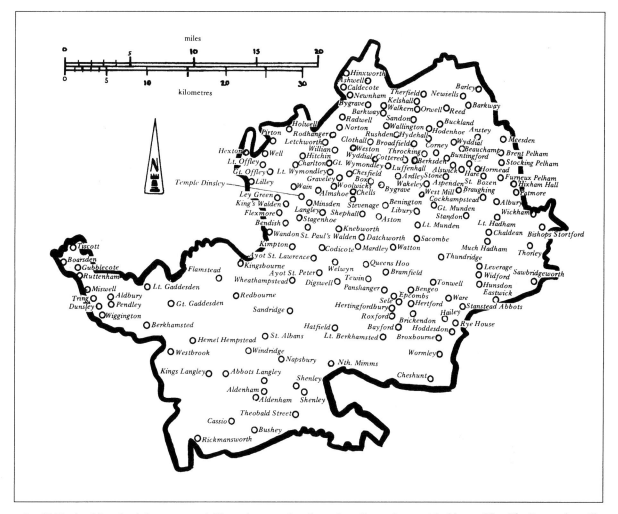

In 1085 the king had important deliberations and exhaustive discussions with his council about this land and how it is peopled and with what sort of men. Then he sent his men all over England into every shire to ascertain how many hundreds of hides of land there were in each shire, and how much land and livestock the king himself owned in the country, and what annual dues were lawfully his from each shire. He also had it recorded how much land his diocesan bishops, his abbots and his earls and ... each man who was a landholder ... had in land and livestock, and how much money it was worth. So very thoroughly did he have his enquiry carried out that there was not a single hide, not one virgate of land, not even ... one ox, nor one cow, nor one pig, which escaped the notice of his survey.

The *Anglo-Saxon Chronicle* exaggerates the completeness and accuracy of the enquiry, which came to be known as the 'Domesday Survey', but it is an astonishing and unique document from which most of our knowledge of England at this time comes—a document all the more amazing for having been compiled, with no precedent or pilot scheme, in the course of one year.

38 *The Domesday vills. Note how they crowd together in the north east. This map should be compared with illustration No10 and No25.*

39 *Domesday entry for Hertford*

The master copy is, we know, an abridgement of the actual information which was collected. Part of the original return for Hertfordshire survives in the document that was concerned with the holdings of the Abbey of Ely, known as the *Inquisitio Eliensis*. As well as listing the questions that the commissioners should ask, it also tells us how the information was collected. In each settlement six villeins, the priest and the reeve (overseer) gave information and swore to its accuracy. In each hundred, or subdivision of the county, a jury of eight—four Frenchmen and four Englishmen—were required to answer questions and to vouch on oath for the accuracy of the record for their area.

The *Inquisitio Eliensis* for Hatfield is as follows:

> The Abbot of Ely holds Hatfield. It answers for 40 hides. Land for 30 ploughs. In lordship 20 hides; 2 ploughs there; a further 3 possible. A priest with 18 villagers and 18 smallholders have 20 ploughs; a further 5 ploughs possible. 12 cottagers; 6 slaves. 4 mills at 47s 4d; meadow for 10 ploughs; pasture for the livestock; woodland, 2000 pigs; from the customary dues of the woodland and pasture, 10s. The total value is and was £25; before 1066 £30. This manor lay and lies in the lordship of the Church of Ely.

A *hide* was enough ground for the upkeep of a family or household—approximately 120 acres. An *acre* was a day's ploughing for one ploughteam, or one strip in the common field, an amount which varies with the nature of the soil and ease of ploughing. A *virgate* was usually a quarter of a hide. A *hundred* was a division of the county that held about 100 households, and which therefore should have been 100 hides; there is, however, abundant evidence of 'rounding off'. Most villages were made to have an exact multiple of five hides. We can imagine the commissioners saying 'Datchworth is a five-hide village' or 'Watton is a ten-hide village'—and adjusting the entries to fit these decisions. The ultimate aim seems to have been to make all the villages in a single hundred add up to 100 hides, as they certainly did for Tring.

40 *Norman arcading at Hemel Hempstead*

Besides the tenants-in-chief and sub-tenants, a number of different classes of men are listed, although it is not always clear how the classes differed, and whether the distinctions are social or economic. In Hatfield the commonest class were the *villeins* who were the villagers who shared the land in the common (open) field, each having an estimated one virgate. They were required to work for the lord on his demesne—his personal holding as *dominus* or master—for part of the time, performing duties defined by manorial custom. *Bordars* and *cottagers* were smallholders, but the differences between them are not clear. The *serfs* were slaves, servants owned by their lords—as were the villeins—but without land of their own. The 'men' in the Ely document were, one must suppose, free men, as were sub-tenants like Robert, since they are not recorded in the main Domesday record that was used for taxation and ownership purposes.

Imperfect and frustrating as the Domesday Survey is, in particular in its predominantly agricultural terms of reference, which offer us only scanty clues as to the existence of towns at this time, it does give us an overall picture the like of which is not available from any other early historical record. It is like an old photograph: the detail may be blurred, and bits of the photographic emulsion missing from the plate, but we can see what it represents.

One hundred and sixty-eight settlements are recorded for Hertfordshire. Only about a quarter of them are south of the River Lea, and the majority seem to be crowded up on the boulder clay of the north-east highlands. One explanation of this might seem to be that in the south-west there are fewer settlements, but with larger populations—but that clearly is not true, since the population density of Edwinstree is more than four times that of Dacorum, and there are four times as many ploughlands in the north-east as in the south-west. To support the conclusion that the difference between the two areas was real, the number of pigs—which were grazed in woodland—tells us that the south-west was covered with forest. It is interesting to compare the maps of the Norman county with the Roman one.

Five towns existed at this time: Hertford, Berkhamsted, St Albans, Ashwell and Stanstead Abbots. The record for Hertford is, unfortunately, both ambiguous and incomplete; it may have had a total population of about one thousand. The other towns had populations approaching five hundred, except for Stanstead Abbots, which had fewer than two hundred inhabitants. The rural population of the county was probably somewhere between twenty and thirty thousand.

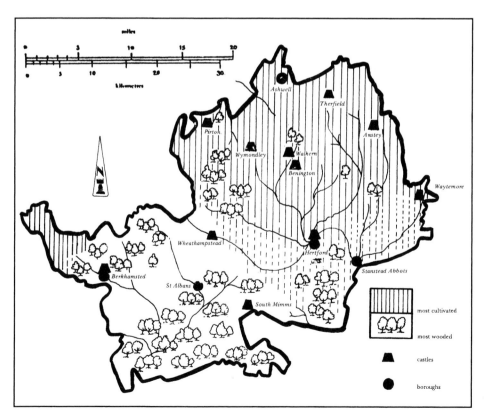

41 *'The location of castles gives us a clue to the principal routes.' In this map of Norman Hertfordshire, the distribution of ploughland was deduced directly from the survey, that of woodland from the number of pigs (which fed on the pannage or mast).*

42 *'Waytemore Castle shows that Stane Street survived at Bishop's Stortford.' An aerial view of the motte, showing the remains of its stone keep.*

Before William the Conqueror died in 1087 he bequeathed his lands in Normandy to his eldest son Robert, and England to his younger son, William (Rufus). A large faction of the Norman lords supported Robert's claim to rule England as well, including Hugh de Grandmesnil, who held Ware; Count Eustace, who held land mainly in the east, and also Tring and Braughing; and Bishop Odo, who held amongst other fiefs, Datchworth and Sacombe. Hugh and Eustace were executed, and their lands confiscated.

During the reign of William Rufus's successor, his younger brother Henry, the main outbreak of castle building began. The original castles at Berkhamsted and Hertford had been sufficient for the subjugation of the Saxons; the invaders were now less concerned to hold down their conquered subjects than to compete with each other. Henry created baronies at Berkhamsted, Benington and Walkern, and new castles were raised at the two new sites. The castle at Berkhamsted was confiscated when its owner William de Mortain rebelled in 1104; it was given to the Chancellor, Ranulph, who repaired and improved it. King Henry held court there in 1123 and also inspected another new castle at Dunstable.

The location of castles gives us clues as to the principal routes in Norman and medieval Hertfordshire. Akeman Street and Watling Street were important, and this was reflected by the positioning of castles at Berkhamsted and Dunstable. Hertford Castle dominated the old valley routes which met and went down the Lea, but which were later easily bypassed at Ware by traffic from the north down Ermine Street. Waytemore Castle shows that Stane Street survived at Bishops Stortford. There was little domestic traffic; most people made few journeys apart from those between home and fields and eventually to market. The landscape was covered by an irregular network of tracks and dragways along the edges of fields and assarts—rights of way with no distant destination, impassable for wheeled vehicles.

43 *Priest seeking sanctuary: from Matthew Paris*

After the death of Henry I, the nobles divided into factions supporting the rival claims of his daughter Matilda, and Stephen, Count of Mortain and Boulogne, who was the son of Henry's sister Adela. In this troubled situation a further rash of castles appeared. Geoffrey de Mandeville, for instance, who became Sheriff of Hertfordshire and was virtually Viceroy for London and Middlesex as well, built a castle at South Mimms, and other castles were thrown up for which we have no documentary evidence at all. Most of them had short lives. As the monarchy regained its strength and authority they were demolished or slighted; Therfield Castle, indeed, was apparently never completed. The official strongholds, however, were allowed to remain. We read of strong garrisons at Hertford and Benington during the crisis period when Richard I was imprisoned in Austria but the latter was slighted in 1212.

By 1213 King John, who had succeeded his brother Richard, had alienated the church, the lords and the people, and in that year a council was summoned at St Albans to discuss his misgovernment. Archbishop Stephen Langton produced a charter of the time of Henry I, which set out the liberties enjoyed by 'free men', who were, of course, far from being the total population of the country at the time. Using this charter as a basis, a draft of a new charter was drawn up, which was later to be called Magna Carta or the Great Charter. Thus it was that St Albans saw 'the birth of the rule of law'. It is interesting to note that this Council of St Albans was also a step on the road towards democratic government, since as well as the lords spiritual and temporal, the reeve and four townsmen from each township on the royal estates were called upon to attend, thus extending the ancient tradition of the 'folkmoot' to a national representative body for the first time.

44 *King John: from Matthew Paris*

Although John reluctantly signed the charter in 1215, he failed to implement it, and Hertfordshire was the principal battleground for the civil war that followed. The king's men, Walter de Godarvil and Waleran the German, held Hertford and Berkhamsted castles and blockaded the roads into London, and the king's army, mainly consisting of mercenaries under the leadership of Falkes de Breauté, ravaged the estates of barons who were hostile to the king. The barons called on the King of France for help. He sent an army under his son, the Dauphin, who then laid waste the lands of the king's adherents. The common people had nothing to gain from either army.

When John died in 1216, the barons found themselves fighting the French. The Dauphin took Hertford Castle after a three-week siege, and Berkhamsted Castle in two weeks. He then occupied St Albans, where the abbot refused to offer him homage as king, but managed to save the town and the abbey from destruction with a bribe of 60 marks. Only a month later Falkes de Breauté pillaged the town, and in his turn had to be bought off; the Dauphin returned a few months later to sack the town on his way to Dunstable.

The reign of Henry III, who inherited the throne as a child, brought little improvement even after the expulsion of the French, since he was continually at war with the barons. Hertfordshire escaped most of the actual conflict, but not the consequent lawlessness. In 1260 the king wrote to the Sheriff of Hertfordshire complaining of 'homicide, robbery and other lawless evildoings' in the latter's domain. However, such events were scarcely surprising when the king's men themselves seemed indifferent to the law. Shortly before, the king's half-brother, who was the Castellan of Hertford Castle, had hunted without permission in the Bishop of Ely's park at Hatfield, raided the manor, and complaining of the quality of the beer and wine which he and his men had stolen, smashed the barrels and 'did endless drunken damage'.

Despite the troubled times, daily life continued in the county as elsewhere in England. Many worked on the land; a smaller, but no less important, proportion chose to make their lives in the growing urban settlements.

45 *The arrival of Louis in 1216; from Matthew Paris*

5

The Medieval Countryside

The feudal villein was a man tied to the soil; the lord 'held' the land, and the people went with it. In return for the strips he held in the open field, the villein was compelled to do services for his lord, as the lord in turn was compelled to do service to the King. At Caddington, for instance, which was partially in Hertfordshire until 1897, the holder of half a virgate in 1222,

> has to work twice a week for the whole year, except Christmas, Easter, and Whitsun; and in each sowing season to plough one-and-a-half acres, or if he has no plough, to do two works. If he ploughs he is quit of one work at that time each week. He must plough one day as 'love earth' in each season. Each virgate which does not plough ought to prepare six quarters of malt or pay six pence, and it shall be quit of six works and shall have fuel for the malt of the lord; those who do not plough shall do the service of carrying five capons or hens to London at Christmas.

The feudal lord regulated the lives of his villeins in other ways than by demanding service. The villein must attend the lord's court, grind his flour at the lord's mill, pay a fine (*merchet*) if his daughter marries, pay another (*leyrwite*) if she becomes pregnant but does not marry, pay an arbitrary poll tax (*tallage*) if his lord decides to impose one; when the tenant of such a holding died, his heirs were obliged to pay a death duty in the form of the best beast (*heriot*) to the lord.

The extract quoted above reveals a tiny loophole which was eventually to be exploited by both man and master: the tenant who paid six pence would be quit of six works. It was thus possible for feudal duties to be commuted on a payment of money. This was the factor which eventually led to the breakdown of the whole system. Commutation of services began in the 13th century; the change was earliest in the south of the county, but was only gradual. On a single manor, one tenant could be paying, whilst another still performed duties. At Codicote (a manor of St Alban's Abbey), the reeve paid 2s. in 1247–'he must pay thirty pence at the four terms *for the works that used to be due*'. Clearly he was now paying rent for his land, rather than giving his labour for it.

Not all services were commuted; it was common for regular weekly works to be commuted into payments, but the extra work at harvest, when whole families worked on the lord's demesne, remained. Commutation was, after all, at the lord's discretion, and equally could be rescinded by him unilaterally, although the 'custom of the manor', the plea that

46 *Making a plough-beam. Tile, c.1340, Tring church*

47 *Harvesting. Tile, c.1340, Tring church*

'we've always done it this way', became a strong force. Even the concept that the villeins were *ascripti glebae* or tied to the land could be subject to commutation, since a fine could be levied on absentees. As early as 1239 a 'fugitive' paid 2s. to his lord at Caldicote, and another gave a pound of pepper in order 'to live outside the lord's liberty'. This payment allowed those technically tied to the land and to agriculture to move to the towns and change their way of life.

Commutation could not have taken place without large quantities of money being in circulation, and the growth of markets can be seen as both the cause and symptom of this. By the end of the 13th century about thirty villages had obtained licences to hold weekly markets. The lord benefited from the tolls he was able to levy on the goods sold, whilst the general economy became more efficient. Village communities, virtually isolated one from another, had only thought in terms of producing crops for self-sufficiency. Markets made it profitable to re-distribute gluts, and to ameliorate the effects of crop failure. Certain communities began to specialise in products particularly suited to their locality; at Caddington and Hitchin, for instance, sheep became the principal agricultural concern.

The maintenance of law and order at the time of the Norman invasion had depended largely on a system of tithing, reflected in the administrative division of the county into hundreds. A tithingman, also known as a *headborough* or *borseholder*, was responsible for the good behaviour of a group of his neighbours—traditionally, ten families, hence 'tithe' or tenth—and in turn he, with nine of his fellows, reported to a hundredman or reeve, who was responsible to the 'shire reeve' or sheriff. In the 11th century the sheriff was effectively the king's deputy in the county, and the most important local instrument of the royal courts.

48 *'A Hundred was a division of the county that held about 100 households.' This map shows the historic hides of Hertfordshire. The hundred of Cashio, somewhat distributed, reflects the widespread holdings of the Abbey of St Albans.*

The hundred court met monthly, to levy taxes and to consider minor criminal and ecclesiastical matters, and twice a year the sheriff was present. By the beginning of the 13th century, the sheriff had delegated part of his responsibility to local lords of the manors, whose reeves held monthly 'customary' courts which were responsible for the day-to-day administration of the manor. The tithingman became 'petty constable', and his duties were codified in the Statute of Winchester in 1285. 'Watch and ward', or the patrolling of the streets with lights to keep an eye on possible lawbreakers at night, was established in towns, and 'hue and cry'—the duty of all citizens to pursue felons and to require

THE HUNDREDS OF HERTFORDSHIRE

1. Dacorum
2. Hitchin Half Hundred
3. Odsey
4. Broadwater
5. Edwinstree
6. Braughing
7. Hertford
8. Cashio

others to assist—was made compulsory. Each hundredman was replaced by two chief constables.

In 1327 Edward III appointed three men to be 'keepers of the peace' for the county of Hertford, and in 1336 he appointed seven men for the same task. In 1361 the Justices of the Peace Act increased their number and also defined and extended their powers. They were chosen from the ranks of the powerful landlords. Eventually the question of whether there was 'a case to answer' in legal terms was decided not by the old hundred juries, but by a grand jury, 'up to twenty-four men of greater quality than the other; chosen indifferently from the whole county by the Sheriff'. From 1350 the justices met four times a year, hence the term 'quarter sessions'. Until 1836 there were separate quarter sessions. Hertford and St Albans for the county, and of the Liberty of St Albans. The justices dealt with minor administrative matters such as licensing and highways at meetings in the hundreds, with only one J.P. present and no jury. These became known as 'petty sessions'. Like the other officers of the manor, such as ale-tasters, constables continued to be elected by manorial courts, although after the 16th century their election had to be confirmed at the quarter sessions. Minor misdemeanours were dealt with locally, but after the mid-15th century presentments for more serious crimes were made to the quarter sessions.

49   *Threshing: from Matthew Paris*

There is little doubt that the parish was treated by its inhabitants with a fierce jingoistic patriotism which is difficult to understand today. A rhyme current in the parish of Welwyn in the early 19th century may well incorporate earlier material: it describes the parish's attitude to its neighbour of Stevenage.

> And onwards to Cave Wood your way you stake,
> Where Stevenage Robbers often did conceal
> What to the World they never dare reveal.
> Long noted Stevenage, where Mothers bawl,
> And to their Scorpion brood, poor things, they call;
> Turnips and Gateposts they are taught to steal
> Soon as the Pap within their mouths they feel.

At Harmer Green the parish boundary went right through a pond. A story is told that a man fell in and was drowning. A local man waded in to save him, but was restrained by his companions, since the unfortunate had tumbled from the 'wrong' side!

During the early Middle Ages the population of the country as a whole seems to have risen rapidly. Caddington, which had 29 tenants in 1086, had at least 85 by 1222, and this appears typical. More people needed more food, which in general could be produced only by taking more land into cultivation. In Hertfordshire land was a limited resource, especially in the north-east of the county, where the villages were very tightly packed, and where even at the time of Domesday there had been very little waste, meadow or woodland. Even the increase of efficiency which was being brought about by the slow breakdown of the feudal system could not wholly relieve the situation, and pressure on resources became so great that natural events that might hitherto have meant hardship could now mean disaster.

These disasters could come in the form of bad weather, animal disease, or human epidemics. Too little rain, or too much at the wrong time, could ruin the crops; something like this must have happened in 1314, since the following summer corn was selling at two-and-a-half times its previous seasonal highest. Among cattle, murrain, which was probably foot-and-mouth, was a serious problem. Although meat production was not seen as so important as arable crops, since it is not as efficient a use of land, oxen were the main beasts of burden and pulled the plough.

In 1341 murrain and bad weather rendered farming almost impossible, and large areas of land were left unploughed, including the greater part of Ashwell, Barkway, Benington, Braughing, Buckland, Bygrave, Clothall, Cottered, Datchworth, Hatfield, Great and Little Hormead, Layston, Meesden, Reed, Rushden, Sandon, Therfield, Totteridge, Wallington, Walkern, Wakeley, Welwyn, Westmill and Wyddial.

In 1348 the Black Death reached England. In Codicote, for example, five tenants died in November of that year, 59 by mid-May of 1349, and a further 25 by December. The total death toll for the county is not known, but a St Albans monk wrote that the pestilence had 'halved all flesh'; in the abbey itself the prior, the sub-prior and 47 other monks died. At Tyttenhanger 31 tenants died, and in the 68 Hertfordshire

50 *'These inscriptions conjure up a powerful picture of the times, with the bewildered survivors of the wrath of God cowering in the church.' The graffiti in Ashwell church tower, recording the Black Death and the great storm of 15 January 1361.*

parishes belonging to the diocese of Lincoln no less than 21 institutions to benefices had to be made in 1349. In the tower of Ashwell church is a deeply-scratched graffito:

MCter Xpenta miseranda ferox violenta
MCCL
Superest plebs pessima testis
('1350, wretched, fierce, violent ... the dregs of the people survive to tell the tale')

The plague returned from time to time, and a further inscription was added in January 1361, after the violent storm on St Martin's Day:

In fine ije
Ventus Validus
MCCCoc anno Maurus in orbe tonat
('At the end of the second [plague] a mighty wind this year Maurus thunders in the heavens 1361')

Further up is added:

Primula Pestis in MterCCC fuit L minus uno
('The first plague was in 1349')

These inscriptions conjure up a powerful picture of the times, with the bewildered survivors of the wrath of God cowering in the church.

The problem of over-population had been solved, albeit in a terrifying way, and this helped to accelerate the social changes which had begun with the commutation of services. Much land became vacant; in 1350, 15 tenements at Codicote were still in the lord's hands, and the solution was tried of combining holdings. Thus the following year Stephen May was granted all the lands late of Robert atte Strete, all the lands of Reginald Alleyn, Edward atte Hache and J. atte Strete for eight-and-a-half years for 20s. a year; 'and Stephen shall do all the service and customs due to the said lands and he may remove one house'. What the 'service and customs' were that Stephen owed his lord are not detailed, but in many instances we have evidence at Codicote that almost any combination of dues might be commuted and retained.

Of five leases granted at one court, two were for rent only; two paid rent, rendered heriot and attended the manorial court; one paid rent, gave boondays and attended the court. Codicote, being part of the notoriously reactionary manor of St Albans, may not be typical, for at Standon, Munden, and Ashwell leases for rent only were being negotiated, and this seems to have been common.

Much of the work on the lords' lands was now being done by paid labour, and the population was now so small that labourers became a valuable and sought-after class. Many of them were technically fugitive from their rightful lords, who might not have offered them such good terms as their new one, but they paid a fine for their absence, and their new manor paid them wages. In 1351 four villeins were fugitive from Codicote, and were at Baldock, Knebworth, Weston and London.

The increased mobility of the population following the Black Death meant that more people were now making longer journeys. For some of

51 *Ashwell church*

52 *Carving on the screen at Sandridge, late 14th century*

53 *Cumberlow Green, a village deserted as a result of the Black Death in the 14th century.*

these the ancient valley roads and surviving lengths of Roman road sufficed, but it often happened that no continuous route existed. The solution was to find the shortest path through the maze of field and farm tracks which existed in response to local requirements. Thus was born 'the roving road, the rolling road, that wanders round the shire'.

The great fall in population in the late 14th century is often associated with the phenomenon of 'deserted villages'. The term is misleading, since it conjures up the picture of a cluster of houses huddled round a church suddenly becoming a ghost town. The nucleated village was in fact exceptional in Hertfordshire; the usual pattern seems to have been that there were a number of hamlets, each set round a small patch of common grazing called a 'green', or if the hamlet was at the extremity of the 'parish', an 'end'. Ardeley, for example, has Church End, Wood End, Gardners End, Moor Green, Munchers Green, Parkers Green, and Wateringplace Green. Church End and Wood End are quite populous today, and there are a few houses at Moor Green; the other original settlements are practically deserted.

It was rare for the plague to kill off *all* the inhabitants of a village at one stroke; what it did more often was to provide the conditions, and the incentive, for accelerating movements of people which had already begun. The new market towns like Buntingford could never have come into existence without the immigration of quite a few people. Survivors of the pestilence were able to move elsewhere in search of better trade, better land, better rents or just because their particular *hamlet*, with its depleted population, was no longer a viable community. So much was shared in the medieval economy, from ploughteams to the services of craftsmen, that there must have been a population level below which the remaining members of a settlement could not manage on their own.

Most of the sixty or so sites that have been suggested as deserted villages in Hertfordshire are in the north-east where there were rich but heavy ploughlands and, although the population density was high, the villages were small. Villages which survived had several greens; those that failed often had only one. One of the smallest of the failed villages, Caldecote, was only 325 acres in extent and its final desertion may have been marked by nothing more spectacular than a family trudging the quarter-of a-mile up the road to Newnham.

In many instances a hamlet moved for reasons not directly connected with the Black Death. Migration often took place from the original greens to a site by a main road, where travellers would provide a ready market for produce, goods and services. At Watton, there were still houses on The Green by the church 50 years ago, although the village was firmly set along the main road at an early period.

Another reason sometimes cited for the disappearance of a village is the creation of a park around the manor house, with the consequent expulsion of the villagers. By the end of the 15th century there were at least forty parks in Hertfordshire, but the making of only one of these led to the destruction of an entire village, at Pendley, near Tring, where

54 *Ardley. C: Church End; Mu: Munchers Green; Mo: Moor Green; P: Parkers Green; Wa: Wateringplace Green; W: Wood End*

55 *'At Pendley, near Tring, Sir Robert Whittingham was granted a licence to enclose 200 acres in 1440. By 1461 the village had gone.' This wild man lies, symbolically, at the feet of Sir Robert's effigy in Aldbury church.*

56 *Arms of the Staple of Calais, Hitchin church*

Sir Robert Whittingham was granted a licence to enclose 200 acres in 1440. By 1461 the village had gone. It was noted in 1506 that 'there were in the town above 13 plows besides divers handicraft men, as tailors, shoemakers and cardmakers, with divers others. The town was afterwards cast down and laid to pasture by Sir Robert Whittingham'.

Many emparkments probably led to the loss of a hamlet, but not of an entire village, as at Digswell, where the mansion and church stood alone until the enlargement of Welwyn Garden City in the 1960s.

Sheep-farming, far less labour-intensive than arable farming, was another cause of desertion of the land which was given a boost by the plague and by the rise in value of broadcloth. Large numbers of sheep were already being grazed at Caddington and Hitchin in the 13th century, and there are records of wool and cloth merchants, as well as fulling mills for finishing cloth, in the county. William Persons of Watford and John Persons of Baldock were shipping wool to Antwerp in 1326, and there are three brasses of 15th-century Merchants of the Staple—the trade organisation which virtually controlled England's wool trade—in Hertfordshire churches, two in Hitchin and one in St Albans Abbey. However, there is only one possible example of a village affected disastrously by a landlord's decision to turn to wool production: Cockenach, a deserted village near Barkway, where the Prior of Royston was grazing 200 sheep by the 15th century.

57 *St Albans Abbey*

6

Church and People

Christianity traditionally first took root in Hertfordshire during the Roman period, and the cathedral and abbey church of St Alban is said to mark the site of the execution of Britain's first Christian martyr. The truth of any legend is hard to establish, but internal evidence suggests that the story first became current in the fourth century, though the events described may have taken place as early as A.D. 209. It seems certain that Christianity was established relatively early in the county, whether or not we choose to accept the traditional story of St Alban.

The legend is that during the persecution of the Christians by the Emperor Diocletian (A.D. 303-4) a pagan citizen of *Verulamium*, a soldier named Alban, sheltered a Christian priest called Amphibalus, and was converted by him. When soldiers came to find the fugitive, Alban changed clothes with his guest and was taken in his stead to the local Roman governor, who was making sacrifices to his gods. Alban refused to join him in this, even though he was offered great inducements to do so, including a bride of noble rank. He was therefore taken to be slain

58 *The execution of Alban: from Matthew Paris*

59 *'A volunteer executioner beheaded him, but as he gave the fatal stroke, his own eyes fell out on the ground.' In this picture by Matthew Paris of the execution of St Alban, the executioner has caught his eyes in his left hand.*

60 *King Offa. Painting over presbytery aisle, St Albans Abbey*

in the arena. When he came to a bridge, it was crowded with spectators, and the river miraculously dried up to allow him to pass dryshod. At the arena, the executioner refused to do his appointed task, and offered himself in Alban's stead. Alban walked out of the arena and up a flower-covered hill. At the top, he caused a miraculous spring to flow, so that he could quench his thirst. A volunteer executioner beheaded him, but as he gave the fatal stroke his own eyes fell out on the ground. Much of the detail, such as the miraculous spring and the drying-up of the river, is common embroidery in the lives of medieval saints. Even the saint's very name is in doubt, since 'Albanus' was a common epithet meaning 'The Briton'.

The place where the martyr had supposedly perished was not forgotten, and in 429, when the Christian bishop Germanus visited Britain, he visited the tomb of Alban. By the middle of the next century, it seems, from a reference to it by the chronicler Gildas, that there was a church on the site which was inaccessible to worshippers, since it was at that time surrounded by pagan Saxon settlers. In his *History of the English Church and People*, the Christian Saxon historian Bede wrote about 730 that there was a church of 'wonderful workmanship', where the sick were healed and miracles performed.

However, the next references to the saint's shrine date from the 13th century, and they conflict with the earlier ones. Roger de Wendover, a monk at the abbey, writing a little before 1236, tells how the abbey was founded by King Offa of the Midland kingdom of Mercia in 793 after he had discovered the tomb of the saint, the site of which had been utterly forgotten—which seems unlikely if Bede is to be believed. Matthew Paris, the abbey historian who succeeded Wendover, lets slip a small but crucial detail: 'Offa, at his own expense, constructed all the buildings except an old edifice which he found, erected formerly out of the ancient edifices of the heathens'.

This would seem to suggest that there was indeed an earlier church on the site. The earliest surviving accounts of the legend support the traditional location of Alban's execution—that is, on a hill 800 yards from the ford outside the gates of the Roman city—for the abbey stands on a hill at just the right distance from the ford at St Michael's.

61 *Saxon baluster shafts in the tower at St Albans Abbey*

In the 12th century Abbot Simon ordered the monk William Marlet to compose lives of the two saints, Alban himself and Amphibalus, which Marlet did, inventing both the biographical details and the sources he quoted to support them. Alban became an important Roman nobleman (and 100 years later a soldier as well). Amphibalus is now said to have escaped to Wales, only to be brought back and martyred with a number of his converts. In 1178 a lay citizen of St Albans named Robert had a vision, as a result of which he discovered what was believed to be the burial place of St Amphibalus on Redbourn Common. (Almost certainly this was a pagan Saxon grave.) The bones were carried reverently to the abbey and re-interred there. The relics of Alban himself are lost, although Danish tradition claims that they were

carried off by marauding Vikings about 860 and can still be seen in the Cathedral of St Alban in Odense.

The first Norman abbot dismissed the building work of his Saxon predecessors as '*rudes et idiotas*' and demolished the existing structures. Using the stockpile of Roman building materials from *Verulamium*, he built the present massive but dull edifice. Only a few monolithic baluster shafts in the triforium of the south transept remain as evidence of the Saxon abbey.

Hertfordshire was the birthplace of the only Englishman to date to have become pope. Nicholas Breakspear was the son of a tenant of St Albans Abbey at Abbot's Langley, who became a monk after the death of his wife, Nicholas's mother. The boy was educated at the grammar school in St Albans, but failed his examination to become a monk at the abbey. However, after travelling abroad, he succeeded in making his mark on the church in a wider sphere, and in 1154 he was elected pope. He apparently bore no ill-will towards the abbey for having rejected him,

62 St Albans from the south east. The abbey is in the centre of the picture, and the great triangular market place stretches to St Peter's, top left.

63 *Building the abbey: from Matthew Paris*

for he not only intervened on its behalf in a dispute with the monks of Ely, but also gave it freedom from the jurisdiction of any bishop, freedom from visitation by a papal legate, and precedence over the Abbey of Westminster. The abbey's grammar school probably existed even before the Norman Conquest. Abbot Geoffrey, who was elected in 1119, had been brought to teach there while still a secular.

Although throughout the Middle Ages there had been small groups of men and women who questioned the practices and religious principles of the Catholic Church, these heretics were mostly quickly crushed. In the 14th century, however, a new kind of opposition to the church appeared, which was not so quickly dealt with. John Wycliffe of the University of Oxford spread the idea that the Bible should be made freely available to all in the vernacular, and eventually completed the first translation from Latin into English. He also criticised the luxury in which some leading churchmen lived, and the emphasis which was placed on worldly goods. Wycliffe's ideas had some powerful patrons, including John of Gaunt, Duke of Lancaster, although Gaunt's stand in the matter was partly dictated by political motives.

Those who adopted Wycliffe's beliefs became known as Lollards, and the movement itself as Lollardy. Despite fierce persecution, and the burning at the stake of a number of Lollard martyrs, the movement remained strong underground. Some Hertfordshire heretics would seem to have confused Lollard beliefs with others which Wycliffe would certainly not have endorsed, like John Gable and John Curteys, who were indicted for heresy in 1452 at Standon. They were said to have maintained that there was no god except the sun and the moon, that no Christian should worship images, and that baptism was unnecessary.

64 *Medieval ecclesiastical boundaries and religious houses.*

By the 13th century St Albans had two dependent cells, the priories at Redbourne and Hertford. There was a Benedictine house at Standon dependent on Stoke in Suffolk, and a priory at Ware dependent on the alien house at St Evroul. Benedictine nuns had been established at Cheshunt, Rowney (Little Munden), Flamstead and Sopwell. The Austin Canons had houses at Royston and Great Wymondley. There were three friaries of comparatively late date established at Langley, Hitchin and Ware in the early 14th century, and a Gilbertine priory was founded at Hitchin in 1361. A mendicant nunnery was set up by Queen Mary at Langley.

In the 12th century there were 11 hospitals in the county, if the

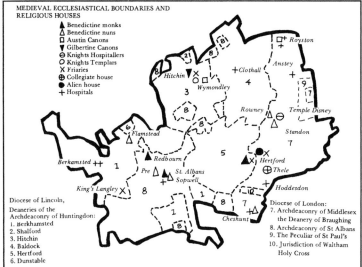

MEDIEVAL ECCLESIASTICAL BOUNDARIES AND RELIGIOUS HOUSES

▲ Benedictine monks
△ Benedictine nuns
▢ Austin Canons
▼ Gilbertine Canons
⊖ Knights Hospitallers
○ Knights Templars
✕ Friaries
⊕ Collegiate house
● Alien house
✛ Hospitals

Diocese of Lincoln,
Deaneries of the
Archdeaconry of Huntingdon:
1. Berkhamsted
2. Shalford
3. Hitchin
4. Baldock
5. Hertford
6. Dunstable

Diocese of London:
7. Archdeaconry of Middlesex
   the Deanery of Braughing
8. Archdeaconry of St Albans
9. The Peculiar of St Paul's
10. Jurisdiction of Waltham
    Holy Cross

one at Royston can be included; that at Hertford became a Maturine friary about 1261, and St Mary de Pre (St Albans) became a Benedictine nunnery in the 14th century. Several hermits are mentioned in the Middle Ages, and the post of anchorite at St Peter's was being advertised in the 15th century.

65 *The 15th-century angel screen, Hitchin*

It might be expected that the drastic alterations to the form and content of church services and the dissolution of the monasteries would produce violent and fierce opposition and social upheaval. This was not the case in Hertfordshire, a fact which deserves some investigation. What was the state of the church at the beginning of the 16th century? Existing evidence would seem to suggest that clergy and people alike were treating it with indifference. Many clerics were absentee—that is, not resident in their parish—or pluralist (holding more than one benefice). There were frequent complaints of disturbances during services; at Kimpton in 1518-19 it was said that babies laughed, cried and even sang in church! Bishop Bonner of London complained of:

> a detestable and abhomynable custume universally Reyning in your parysshes the younge people and other yll desposed personnes dothe use upon Sondayes and hollydayes in tyme of dyvine service and preaching the worde of God to resorte unto Alehouses, and theyre exercyseth unlawful games with greate swearying, blasphemye and drunkennes and other enormyties.

Many of the reforms which were introduced under Henry VIII and his son Edward VI were for the better. After 1541, for instance, every church had to possess a Bible 'of the largest and greatest volume to be had'; by this time the Bible would have been in English. However, the more radical reforms introduced under the influence of the Duke of Northumberland, who exercised the real power as King Edward was only a child, were not all popular. In 1547, it was ordered that all shrines, pictures and 'monuments of superstition' should be removed. This led to some confusion: what was the difference between a monument of religion and one of superstition? The churchwardens at Bishops Stortford got round the problem by commissioning John Laxton to hire a horse and go to London 'for to vew the other churches ther'. With his observations to guide them, they subsequently spent two days 'takyng downe the thyngs in the Roode loft' and sold the church plate and vestments, the latter raising the large sum of £6.

The Hertfordshire religious houses vanished quietly in an atmosphere of uncertainty and indifference. When the King's agents came to suppress the priory of St Mary de Pre, there was nobody there; the prioress had died and the remaining five nuns had just walked away. Some members of religious houses played an active rôle in the suppression, like Richard Ingworth, prior of Kings Langley, who was given the priory and its possessions as his own property and later became Bishop of Dover.

66 *Rebus or punning arms of de Wheathampstead, St Albans Abbey*

At the end of 1539, Richard Boreman, the abbot of St Albans, surrendered the abbey to the King. There were only 38 monks left who were all given pensions. The abbey itself became simply a parish church. The lady chapel housed the grammar school, which was separated from the church by a passageway right through the structure from north to south. The parish could not afford to maintain the whole of the building, and by the 19th century only the presbytery and part of the north transept were in use.

The origins of many grammar schools are unknown, and some, including one at Stevenage as well as that of St Albans, existed in medieval times. It was during and following the dissolution of the monasteries and chantries that many wealthy people were prompted to found or to endow existing schools, to ensure that the children of the poor might receive a godly upbringing. The school could also be a surrogate chantry. Thomas Alleyn's will in 1558 required the scholars of Stevenage to pray 'for me their founder morning and evening'.

67 *The ancient parishes of Hertfordshire. These, and the hundreds, form a basis for much of the historic record of the county.*

The policies of the Protestant nobility who had dominated English religious life during the reign of Edward were reversed at the accession of Edward's older sister, Mary. It was not possible to restore all the church lands to their original owners, but she did attempt to restore the old forms of service and to bring England back within the Catholic church.

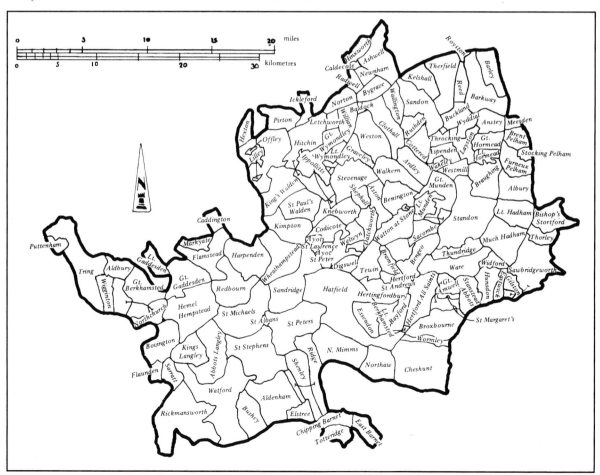

Six years after they had taken down their 'monuments of superstition', the churchwardens of Bishops Stortford were busy 'making up' an altar, constructing a rood screen, buying crosses, incense boats, and stands and 'stuff' for a new surplice. Although we do not have information for the whole of the county, there is reason to believe that the incumbents of Ayot St Lawrence, Barkway, Braughing, Broxbourne, Bushey, Datchworth, Little Hormead, Puttenham, Royston, Rushden, Westmill and Wallington were all dismissed from their livings because they had 'married or otherwise slanderously disordered or abused themselves'. In 1555 three Hertfordshire 'heretics', who refused to abandon Protestantism, were burnt at the stake: they were William Hale at Barnet, Thomas Fust at Ware and George Tankerville at St Albans—on 'Romeland'.

68   *Braughing*

After five years of Mary's restored Catholic church, she was succeeded in 1558 by her Protestant sister Elizabeth, and the church furniture and incumbents started another shuffle. Tables replaced altars and 'superstitious monuments' like roods were demolished. A number of Hertfordshire priests were dismissed for their adherence to the 'old learning', although information on this point is incomplete.

It is astonishing to learn that many parish incumbents had little or no learning of any kind. For example, in the deanery of Braughing, which seems to be typical, of 29 beneficed clergy, only nine were graduates. At this time Latin was the basis of a Grammar School education, yet eleven were said to have a 'slight or middling' knowledge of Latin, and three had no Latin at all. Eighteen were described as having 'a slight or middling knowledge' of theology. Elizabeth's bishops, under the leadership of the new archbishop, Matthew Parker, started a programme of clerical education with regular 'homework' to be submitted for inspection by the less-educated ministers:

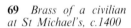

69   *Brass of a civilian at St Michael's, c.1400*

> Every minister of this jurisdiction, being no preacher or master of Artes shall monethly geve under his owne hand an exposition of one Chapter of St Pawle to the Romans begenninge at the first Chapter and so goeinge forwarde monethly ... and so to be delivered quarterly to the judge ... to that ende that it may appeare how they have profyted in their studyes.

The Elizabethan ecclesiastical authorities not only had to struggle with the opposition of Catholics and the poor quality of many of their clergy; they also had to contend with those who felt the restrained version of Protestantism maintained by Elizabeth and Parker was unsatisfactory. The authority of the church was flouted by the omission of prescribed rites and ceremonies at will by those ministers who wanted a more radically changed Church of England. They believed that the minister should not be so firmly under the control of a bishop, and some were for some degree of self government by the members of individual congregations. Those who held these ideas were, however, mainly university-trained clergymen; as yet 'Puritanism', as this movement was beginning to be called, had had little impact on the laity. An example of an Elizabethan Hertfordshire Puritan was William Dyke, the incumbent

70 *The font at Ware,
c.1400*

of St Michael's in St Albans, of whom it was said he was 'troubling his auditors with new opinions and notions, thwarting the established religion'. His superiors eyed him with suspicion, but he did not suffer any very harsh punishment for his views.

When, at Elizabeth's death, she was succeeded by James VI of Scotland, who now became James I of England, many Puritans hoped that a more Puritan form of worship would be introduced. The Church of Scotland adhered to Presbyterianism, which was a form of Protestantism without bishops, and was generally more strictly 'reformed' than its sister church in England. James had not been crowned a year before he was being petitioned unofficially by local clergy who accosted him when he was hunting at Royston. Other more official pleas followed.

As the monarch was the supreme head of the Church of England, the Puritans hoped he could be persuaded to overrule the bishops. However, James was in fact far more in sympathy with the English than with the Scottish form of Protestantism, and had no intention of significantly altering the moderate forms of worship which Elizabeth had established. His stand on the matter quickly became clear when he issued directions limiting the matters which might be discussed in sermons to the Creed, the Catechism, the Commandments and the Lord's Prayer, and forbidding 'popular auditory' of 'deep points' of theology.

If King James had refused to depart significantly from the Elizabethan settlement of the church, his son Charles was noticeably more sympathetic towards a more ritualistic and impressive form of church service—a tendency which greatly alarmed many of his subjects, despite the king's own loyalty to Protestantism. In 1633 Charles appointed a new archbishop of Canterbury, William Laud, whose name was to become synonymous with a movement amongst certain bishops and clerics for a more beautiful and a more strictly controlled Church of England. In many cases the 16th-century abolition of 'superstitious monuments' and the dissolution of the monasteries had led to a lack of respect for ecclesiastical buildings of any kind. Many churches were in a bad state of repair, requiring not only redecoration but basic structural work, and this was one area in which Laud's agents attempted to achieve an improvement.

However, attempts were also made to halt the tendency which had developed to emphasise the sermon as the main attraction of a church service, and to reintroduce an atmosphere of reverence and worship. Ministers were instructed to wear proper vestments, instead of their ordinary clothes; and the communion table, generally sited in the main aisle at this time where it was often utilised as a convenient place to leave hats and cloaks, was ordered to be removed to the east end of the church and railed off from ill-usage. Many clerics and laymen felt this to be a disguised kind of Popish altar, and refused to co-operate, like Charles Chauncy, the vicar of Ware, who refused, until admonished by his bishop, to be present at the consecration of the private chapel of Thomas Fanshawe of Ware Park. He also told his churchwardens that he would 'leave the place' if they set up a 'communion table with a rail'. When he heard that they had actually authorised this to be done, he 'used reproachful speeches ... and affirmed that it was an innovation, a snare to men's consciences, a breach of the second commandment, and an addition to God's worship'. In 1635 he was found guilty of contempt of 'the ordinary and the jurisdiction ecclesiastical' and of 'raising a schism and distraction in the parish of Ware'. He recanted, but eventually, unable to force himself to adhere to the practices demanded of him, emigrated to America, where he became the first president of Harvard College.

Chauncy was one of a large number—exactly how many is uncertain—who set out from Hertfordshire to find freedom of worship in the New World. Among the earliest names recorded are those of Ezekiel and Susanna Richardson, who left Westmill in April 1630. They settled at first at Charlestown, and later became founder settlers of the town of Woburn. John and Jacob Eliot from Widford were among several members of their family to emigrate. In 1646 John Eliot preached to the Indians in their own tongue, the first time this had been done, and in 1653 he published the first book in that language, a *Catechism*. Among the other works of this great scholar, who was one of the founders of Harvard, were translations into the Indian language of the New and Old Testaments.

In 1633 Samuel Stone took his wife and three daughters on *The Griffin* to New England. They settled initially at Newtown (later to be renamed Cambridge) before moving on to found a settlement called Hartford, after Stone's town of origin. Estimates vary of the number of Puritans who left St Albans. In 1635 *The Planter* carried at least eighteen (perhaps as many as forty) to Boston and *The Defence* carried Robert Long, his wife and his nine children by a previous marriage to Charlestown.

After the outbreak of civil war in England in 1642, the ecclesiastical government collapsed. Archbishop Laud and other bishops were in prison; and some emigrants chose to return home. Soldiers of the Parliamentary army took the opportunity to uproot altar rails and destroy any traces of decoration or popery which had survived, an action which was often tacitly approved of by the local people. At Hadham in 1640 following the destruction of the altar rail and the painted windows, the soldiers responsible 'might easily have been prevented and apprehended, had not the town connived at it'. After the victory of Parliament, committees were set up to examine complaints against 'scandalous ministers', who were in some cases poor specimens indeed, but in others probably simply the victims of some local grudge. These men lost their livings and were replaced by Puritans, sometimes by former emigrants to America.

The establishment of the Commonwealth did not mean that religious toleration was introduced. 'High church' ministers who were unwilling to change their views were replaced by Puritans. The principal targets of persecution in Hertfordshire were the Baptists and the Quakers. In 1643 the minister at Hemel Hempstead was sent to Newgate for 'anabaptist

71 *Oliver Cromwell*

teachings', and the following year another preacher there was described as 'an ecclesiastical socialist and anarchist opposed to infant baptism'. By the mid-1650s there were Quaker communities established at Bishop's Stortford and Hertford; their refusal to pay tithes, a refusal in which they were not unique but particularly determined, brought upon many of them the seizure of their goods or spells in prison.

With the restoration of Charles II to the throne in 1660, another ecclesiastical upheaval took place. At least forty parsons were dismissed. At Barley the incumbent expelled by the Parliamentary Committee for Scandalous Ministers was restored; the displaced Puritan became a 'public preacher' at Royston, preaching on market days until silenced by the Act of Uniformity in 1662. The virtual collapse of ecclesiastical authority during the years of the war had led to the appearance of a multitude of different religious sects; Oliver Cromwell's Protectorate had taken stern measures to try to restrain the more extreme of these, and they were naturally even less popular with the bishops who were now restored to their former power. In 1661, 22 Quakers were sent to prison in Hertford; the diarist Pepys commented that in Baldock 'the Quakers do continue and rather grow than lessen'. Other religious nonconformists continued to flourish in Hertfordshire, despite the persecution of authority: John Bunyan preached at Preston and Coleman Green, and other 'hedge preachers' also drew great crowds.

72 'Spencer Cowper was tried at Hertford assizes in 1699 for murder ... was made a judge and was mercifully inclined when he presided over trials for murder. ... His monument in Hertingfordbury church shows him in judge's robes between Prudence and Justice.'

Nonconformity had in fact come to stay, albeit for many years in as discreet a fashion as possible: the more successful sects began to acquire permanent meeting-places for themselves. The Baptists at Hitchin acquired a barn for this purpose, and the Hertford Quakers built themselves a meeting house which is the oldest to have been in continuous use. After the Declaration of Indulgence in 1672, which allowed a measure of freedom of worship, there was a spate of chapel building.

A scandal in the late 17th century showed, however, how strong the feeling of many still was against Dissenters. Spencer Cowper (grandfather of the poet, William) was tried at Hertford Assizes in 1699 for the murder of Sarah Stout, who had probably drowned herself after being rejected by him. His defence, apart from a refutation of the foolish medical evidence, rested upon two assertions: that the Quakers, of whose community the Stouts were leading members, had brought the case to remove the stigma of the coroner's verdict of suicide, and that the case had been fomented by the Tories to discredit the Whigs at the forthcoming Hertford election, and wrest the borough from the Cowpers. Ultimately the Tories took the borough seat, but Spencer 'resumed his practice at the bar, was elected Member of Parliament for Bercalstone, was made a Judge, and was mercifully inclined when he presided over trials for murder'. His monument in Hertingfordbury church shows him in judge's robes between Prudence and Justice.

73 *John Bunyan*

7

Medieval Towns, Trade and Industry

In the Middle Ages, as throughout most of its history, Hertfordshire was predominantly rural. Even the villages were mainly dispersed (see Chapter 5), and there were few centres that were sufficiently urban to justify the name of 'town'. This term is probably best applied to those centres which not only possessed substantial market places, but also contained resident craftsmen and merchants dependent upon the existence of a market, rather than simply fulfilling local needs: in short, boroughs *de facto*, whatever their legal status.

Since landlords wished to reap the benefits of trade, they deliberately created new market towns, strategically placed on main roads. The Knights Templar built Baldock where two Roman roads crossed on the Icknield Way in about 1140, and there is a tradition that the name of the town came from *Baudacum*—the Latinised form of Baghdad. The Canons of St Rohesias's [Lady Roysie's] Cross were granted a market in 1189, and the town of Royston grew up in no less than five parishes, a situation which persisted until it became a parish in its own right in 1540. It was in both Cambridgeshire and Hertfordshire until 1897! Chipping Barnet (the word 'chipping' or 'ceiping', from which we derive 'cheap', means a market) was built by the Abbey of St Albans after the grant of a market in 1199.

Not all the markets that were planted and nurtured by landlords necessarily took root, and the developments at Buckland, south of Royston, show how important the selection of the site was. In 1252 the manor of Pope's Hall obtained a charter for a market, and a new settlement—Chipping—was created. Clearly it was not a great success, and six years later the village of Buckland obtained a similar charter for a weekly market and a three-day fair. The really strategic location, however, was just a bit further south, where the road from the Pelhams crosses Ermine Street, and a settlement called Buntingford began to develop here spontaneously. Eventually Elizabeth de Burgh of Pope's Hall transferred the market to Buntingford in 1360.

In addition to those mentioned in Domesday, other towns had obtained borough status, at least insofar as their tenants had special privileges in connection with holding land in the town. The Bishop of London exploited the obviously important location of Stortford and fostered its privileges. Standon, Hemel Hempstead and Sawbridgeworth

74 *Hemel Hempstead church*

probably became boroughs, and Watford appears as a market in the reign of Henry II. Hitchin was referred to as a borough in 1248, and the 'farm of the borough' (the profits paid to its lord) were worth eight and a half marks in 1268.

In 1156 it was granted to the royal borough of Berkhamsted that all its 'men and merchants'—a distinction which suggests the existence of mercantile gilds —'should have the King's firm peace throughout all his lands of England and Normandy, and should be granted all the laws and customs which they had at the time of Edward the Confessor, William the First and Henry the First ... withersoever they went with their merchandise throughout England, Normandy, Aquitaine and Anjou, and should be quit of toll, pontage, passage and piccage, pannage and stallage, suits of shires and hundreds, aids of sheriffs and serjeants, geld, Danegeld, hidage, blodewhite and bredwhite, murders and other things related to murders, works of castles, walls, ditches, parks and bridges, and all secular custom and servile work'.

Another town to achieve borough status was Ware, which, although further north than Hertford, because of the river diversion mentioned in Chapter I, was both downstream of it and closer to London both by water and by road, since Ermine Street followed the valley. Ware was also central to the rich corn-growing ploughlands of the north east. It

75 Aerial view of Hitchin from the south. The triangular area in the centre is the original market place, in which permanent shops have replaced the original market stalls.

76 Brent Pelham cottages

77 *The seal of the Borough of Hertford*

was granted a market in 1199, and Robert, Earl of Leicester, granted his tenants free burgage for 2s. per annum.

The royal borough of Hertford had been given monopolies over navigation on the River Lea, and control of the crossings at Hatfield, Ware and Thele (Stansted St Margarets), but its geographical position had been determined more by considerations of military strategy than by those of economic viability. In 1247 the burgesses of Hertford complained that the inhabitants of Ware were passing freely over the ford and the bridge without payment of tolls, and were literally forestalling Hertford by holding illegal markets on Hertford's own market-days, Wednesday and Saturday, as well as on their own legitimate day, Tuesday. To make matters worse, the citizens of London had built their own granaries at Thele, and were using their own boats for transport, rather than those of Hertford! In 1275 Ware constructed weirs in the river to obstruct navigation to Hertford, and diverted the king's highway between the towns.

In consequence of this competition, Hertford declined and in the 14th century was actually referred to as 'Hertford-by-Ware'. However, the castle continued to be a favourite royal dwelling, and the burgesses maintained their ancient rights and privileges. In the 15th century, we read of them controlling the transfer of land within the borough, which, since its holding conferred special status upon the tenant, could only pass freely between burgesses. There was the equivalent of a corporation in the 'chief pledges', a small group of burgesses who elected, as well as their own members, the officials of the borough: the bailiff, sub-bailiff, two constables, two weighers of bread, two supervisors of meat, two supervisors of fish and two supervisors of hides.

The successive abbots of St Albans were largely responsible for the destruction of *Verulamium*, the older settlement alongside which their own new town had grown up. In 948 the sixth abbot, Ulsinus, built three churches at the entrances to the towns—St Peter's, St Michael's and St Stephen's. The latter two are on Watling Street, and St Michael's stands on the site of the Roman forum. Traffic was diverted from the Roman road through the Norman town, and the Roman settlement was systematically plundered for building materials. It was regarded as the 'hiding-place of robbers, body-snatchers and evil women'.

78 *The settlements at St Albans: V=Verulamium, Roman; K=Kingsbury, Saxon; SA=St Albans, Norman and later; Sm=St Michael's; SS=St Stephens's; Sp=St Peter's; C=Abbey. The diverted route of Watling Street through the market is shown. The old course is shown by a dashed line.*

The destruction of *Verulamium* may be seen as the removal by the abbey of a possible competitor for the trade which it wanted for its own new town. Another competitor was the fortified Saxon borough of Kingsbury (King's Borough), which lay on high ground on the opposite side of the Ver from *Verulamium*, and right next door to St Albans. Aelfric, the seventh abbot, bought the great pool which stretched from St Michael's to Holywell and drained it, thus depriving the inhabitants of Kingsbury of the fish from which many of them earned their living. The borough declined after this, and King Canute allowed the abbey to demolish all its buildings except one, which was left standing as a token of royal possession. The site was finally cleared in the reign of Stephen. Fishpool Street and Kingsbury Mill remain to remind us of this vanished

settlement, and the boundary of St Albans excluded the Kingsbury area until the 19th century.

The peculiar feature of the medieval history of St Albans was its running battle with the abbey for the right to self government. The abbots took the view that the citizens were villeins; they themselves insisted that they were free men. Two particular issues aroused hot feelings: the claim by the townspeople to independent representation in Parliament by burgesses, in addition to the abbot's own seat as a spiritual lord; and the abbey's claim to a monopoly of all milling facilities. In 1327 the townsmen besieged the abbey, demanding that the abbot surrender to them certain charters which they claimed had granted them privileges at the time of the Norman Conquest. A royal proclamation was just in time to prevent an actual assault on the Holywell Gate; subsequently an arbitration panel of local lawyers and knights confirmed the townsmen's rights to all the liberties they demanded—except those of milling.

79 *A Norman and a Saxon: from Matthew Paris*

The abbey, however, did not consider the matter closed and, after a series of further incidents and appeals to royal authority, the abbot charged the burgesses of St Albans with extorting the charter of rights, with armed assault against the abbey, breaches of the peace, and with conspiracy. In 1332 the town was forced to surrender its hard-won charters, and even to pay 200 marks damages to the abbey. As a token of his renewed control over milling, the abbot is said to have collected in all the querns in the town and had them set in the floor of his parlour as a memento!

Even now the quarrel did not die: it merely slumbered, waiting a chance to break out again. The chance was provided by the Peasants' Revolt of 1381. At the news of the outbreak of the rebellion in Kent, the townsmen of St Albans seized the chance to pursue their own particular ends. William Grindecobbe, a member of a leading family in the town, took the lead, and informed the abbot that Wat Tyler, the Kentish leader of the revolt, had promised that 20,000 men would destroy the abbey if the abbot did not permit the townspeople to join him. The abbot complied, even sending his own servants and esquires to accompany the Hertfordshire rebels as they marched on London, pillaging as they went. The frightened royal government, acting on behalf of the boy king Richard II, granted the rebels freedom or manumission from their feudal lords, and the St Albans rebels returned home with this written promise in their hands. The abbot confirmed the manumission of his 'villeins', and, after further threats from the mob, which was now attacking abbey property, granted rights of pasture, chase and fishing, and freedom from interference in the government of the town.

Similar rights were granted to the manors of Abbots Langley, Watford, Hertford, Berkhamsted, Redbourn, Tring, Codicote, Shephall, Newnham, Aston, Northaw, Sandridge, Tyttenhanger, Cassiobury, Walden, Norton and Hexton. However, the main forces of the rebellion under Tyler and Jack Straw were defeated at London by the king's

80   *The south end of St Albans market place*

soldiers, and Sir Walter atte Lee was sent to St Albans to restore order. With great difficulty he managed to capture Grindecobbe and the other leaders of the revolt and sent them to Hertford; they were hanged, drawn and quartered. Many others were imprisoned—one chronicler thought about eighty—but it seems that they were released during the following winter. An enquiry ruled that all the services previously due to the abbey should be restored, and the charters revoked. The revolt was crushed; but mysterious outbreaks of arson directed against abbey property, and resistance to abbey control of the town, persisted and occasionally led to open confrontation thereafter.

What would a medieval Hertfordshire town have looked like? Originally the market place was simply an open space, usually triangular, and analogous to a village green. Church and public buildings adjoined the market place, and the long thin holdings of the townsmen (portmen, burgesses or freemen) crowded together, each with a narrow frontage onto the market place. Temporary stalls were set up, usually once a week, in the open space, but increasingly from the 14th century more permanent structures were permitted, which eventually became shops and houses, usually with narrow alleyways between them, commemorating the original rows of stalls. The modern plan of an ancient town such as St Albans or Hitchin exhibits in this way the fossilised layout of its market.

Within the town, and within the market itself, traders and craftsmen specialising in particular goods tended to congregate together, and from the records we can often deduce where they worked and traded. At St Albans, we read of the 'flesh shambles' where the butchers were found, the fish market, the 'women's market' for dairy produce, wheat 'cheaping', the 'pudding shambles', and the 'leather shambles'. French Row was formerly Cordwainers' Row, where the shoemakers could be found.

The various crafts or 'mysteries' co-operated in the formation of gilds or brotherhoods, which were essentially a kind of trades union for the regulation of their internal affairs, and the maintenance of their monopoly over their particular business. Expensive and lengthy apprenticeships were needed to qualify a young applicant for membership. The gilds often also had a religious dimension and were associated with chapels, chantries and charities. They also performed mystery plays, although no cycle survives from Hertfordshire. In 1443 'was at seint albons the last of juyn a play of Eglemour and Degreballe'. Miracle plays were also performed, and St George was a favourite subject. The largest known production, at Royston in 1511, involved a combined effort by 28 parishes in North Hertfordshire and Cambridgeshire. A processional dragon was kept at Bishop's Stortford; churchwarden's accounts at the end of the 15th century noted its repair, and its hiring out to other parishes.

Market towns were usually at least eleven miles apart; produce was usually only transported about five miles at most. Competition was further avoided by holding markets on different days. In addition to the weekly markets, many places were granted the right to hold fairs or

V   *Aerial view of St Albans from the north east. In the background is Prae Wood, the site of the first (Belgic) settlement. Below that, behind the lake is the Roman city of Verulamium. To the right of this is the Saxon Burgh, Kingsbury. The Norman town with its long triangular market place and parallel burgage plots lies between St Peter's Church and the Abbey.*

VI   *The Rainbow Portrait of Queen Elizabeth I in Hatfield House. The painting is attributed to Isaac Oliver.*

VII *Ashridge. Originally a college of Bonhommes, this was the home of Elizabeth I during Mary's reign. The present gothick house, now a management college, was built by James and later Jeffrey Wyatt 1808-1820 in Totternhoe stone. The spire is a modern replacement in resin-bonded fibreglass.*

VIII *Hatfield House from the air. It was built in 1611 — the hall of the original palace is on the left.*

grand markets, which usually lasted three days, the middle one being a feast day. To these came traders, entertainers and other visitors, often from great distances. Consumer protection was a problem, and courts of summary justice were set up because many of the cases involved temporary inhabitants, the travellers, the *pieds poudreux* or men of dusty feet, who gave the courts their common name of 'pie powder courts'.

The form of government in a market town depended upon its individual history and status. True boroughs were regulated by their freemen, as at the 'portmoot' at Berkhamsted. Where a market had been granted to the landlord, the town's affairs were still in the hands of the manorial court. Hitchin is an interesting case. In the 13th and 14th centuries it is referred to as a borough, although no burgage rents are recorded, and no member of parliament returned by it. It was governed by its manorial court, which even into the 20th century was called the 'baron court of the Manor of Hitchin Portman and Foreign'. Portmen were those living as freemen within the bounds of a borough; foreigners lived within the manor, but outside the borough. As well as electing a bailiff and such standards officers as ale-conners, weighers of bread and leather searchers, the court appointed constables 'for the town' and 'for the foreign'.

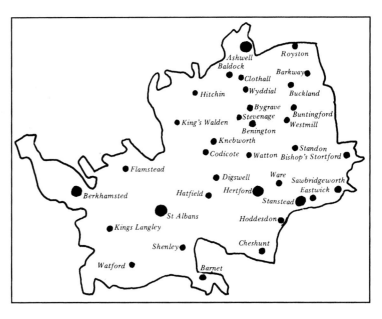

81 'Market towns were usually at least 11 miles apart.' Distribution of medieval boroughs (large dots) and markets (small dots).

Hertfordshire was predominantly a rural county; whilst it possessed its share of craftsmen like saddlers, coopers, wheelwrights and so on, few of its industries had national importance. The two most important occupations, without doubt, were the production of malt from barley, and its subsequent fermentation into ale and beer. These processes were performed everywhere, but especially centred in the north-east of the county, along with the adjoining areas of Bedfordshire and Cambridgeshire, the best barley-growing area. The area around Ware, Stanstead Abbots and Hoddesdon has been described as the 'cradle of the malting industry in England'. Numerous 19th-century maltings can still be seen, particularly near navigable waterways. They are usually long, low buildings, characterised by the conical or pyramidal roof of the kiln, looking not unlike a Kentish oast-house, which projects upwards through the roofline of the main block. The industry is now defunct in Hertfordshire, and many of the maltings are vanishing, since the usually restricted head-space between floors mitigates against conversion to other purposes.

As with many trades, legal records provide the first references to malting. In 1339 the bailiff of Ware was instructed to restore 12 quarters

82 Wool merchant's mark, late 14th century, Hitchin church, south porch

83 *Bushel and strike for measuring malt*

84 *Old and new — and obsolete. The 19th-century maltings on the left were made obsolete in the 20th by the new deep-bed process carried out in those on the right which, in their turn, closed down in 1995.*

85 *'Numerous maltings can be seen, particularly near navigable waterways.' Sawbridge with brewery and maltings beside the Stort Navigation.*

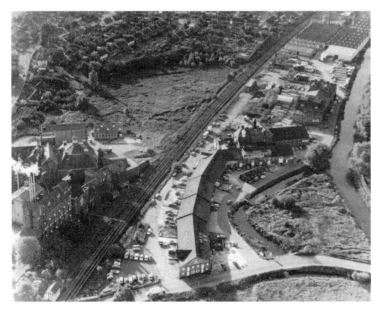

of malt which had been illegally seized to Raymond Peregrine. This malt was taken in transit, which indicates that considerable amounts were being carried. In the 1470s we find Robert Mascall, a maltman of Aldenham who was accused of abduction, regularly visiting London 'as he must nedys do wekely by cause of this occupacion'.

Brewing was an essential and universal process from the earliest times, and, unlike malting, could be a household activity. It always seems to have been subject to rates and regulations, and is frequently referred to in court and borough rolls, as, for example, when 79 brewers were fined at St Albans in 1355. Most of them, significantly, also had other trades.

At the time of Domesday, every village had its mill, driven by water or wind, and by the late 16th century the county was 'stocked beyond its needs with mills working for London'. Originally mills ground flour, but of course the power could be used for other ends, and watermills were converted to other uses, or even constructed for them. The mechanical fulling of cloth—that is to say, beating it in water to clean and tighten the loose weave of newly-woven wool—was invented in the 12th century. The abbot of St Albans converted a number of watermills on abbey estates for fulling; these were the cause of one of the frequent disputes between town and abbey in 1266, when the townsmen challenged the abbey's monopoly.

There were early fulling mills at Braughing, Gilston, Berkhamsted, Hemel Hemstead (in the parish of Codicote) and Welwyn, and fullers are also mentioned elsewhere. The period for which any mill functioned as a fulling mill cannot be determined; none was performing this function after the end of the 17th century.

The fulling process could be readily adapted to the pulping of rags for paper, and Hertfordshire paper was made from a very early date. John Tate, son of a Lord Mayor of London, owned the first recorded paper mill in England at Hertford. Although the exact site is unknown, there is a Papermill Mead to the north of the town. In an edition of *De Proprietatibus Rerum* of Bartholomeus Anglicus, printed by Wynkyn de Worde about 1495, appears the following: 'And John Tate the younger Ioye mote he broke whiche late hathe in Englond doo makes this paper thynne That now in our Englysshe this boke is printed Inne'.

Tate's paper was also used for the *Golden Legend*, and for an edition of Chaucer, both printed in 1498, in which year Henry VII visited Tate's mill when staying at Hertford Castle. The making of fine paper was a craft of national importance. A large papal bull issued by Alexander VI in 1494, and a supplement to it published a year later, both employ Tate's product. It seems likely, however, that the mill could not compete with foreign imports, since his will left the bulk of his estates to his eldest son, but instructed that his executors should sell the mill 'to moste advantage'.

86 *'Every village had its mill, driven by water or wind.' There are no commercial mills in the county today, so the wheel of Redbournbury mill is now a monument to a past age.*

87 *Tate's watermark*

During the 1480s the 'Schoolmaster Printer' had been producing books at St Albans. His name is not known, and he has been nicknamed 'John Insomuch', using the opening word of one of his books as a surname. His work begins only just after that of Caxton. The books he printed included *On the Elegance of Cicero and the Exotic Words in his fruitful Rhetoric; Nova Rhetorica; A Chronicle of England*; and the famous *Boke of St Albans*, as well as others, between about 1480-88.

If they are properly maintained for the purpose, even quite small streams can be used to carry heavy loads from place to place, and it is clear that the Romans made great use of water transport. The most important natural waterway in Hertfordshire is the river Lea, which linked the rich grain-producing lands of north-east Hertfordshire and the adjacent counties with London. In 1220 we find that Margaret, Countess of Winchester, made a grant to the Canons of the Holy Trinity for the passage of corn from Ware to London. In 1300 the inhabitants of Ware, perhaps recalling the exploits of King Alfred, blocked the river to prevent Hertford from competing for trade, and it seems that the blockage was still there 150 years later.

Boatmen, however, are not the only users of a river, and can find themselves in competition with others, particularly millers. In 1482 a commission heard that

> The head of the entry of the Abbot of Waltham's Myll were water goeth out of the Kynges Streame is of xvj foote broade where it should be but fower foote by which the Kynges Streame is soe hurt. Also the said Abbott hath a Locke which is but xvj foote broade where it should be xviij foote for which cause it must be broken upp for it is great jeopardy to alle manner of Barges and Boates that goe uppon the Water.

At this time a 'locke' would have been a gap in a weir, fitted with removable paddles; a boat could pass through when the paddles were removed, on a surge of water, and for this reason this type of lock is called a 'flash lock'.

We can still descry the shape of the medieval towns in our modern conurbations, and picture from contemporary records and illustrations what daily life was like. Little of the architecture remains. The churches usually do survive, with alterations, and it may be possible to recognise gildhalls—the meeting-places of the gildsmen—under such guises as the former W.H. Smith's at St Albans, and Brotherhood House at Hitchin. The town houses and shops were all timber-framed, with daub infill, since there was little stone and no brick available locally. Some timber-framed buildings do survive concealed behind modern façades, and the author's own house (see plates 88 and 89), despite its Georgian windows and brick nogging, gives some idea of the sort of house which a well-to-do medieval person could have built.

The interior of medieval houses can be imagined from surviving objects, and from contemporary wills and inventories. In 1437 Alice atte Welle left, amongst other things, 'three cusshons of work rede and grene, a pot with smal feet, a cofer that was my mothers to lay her kerchiefs in' as well as a bed with a religious painting on it, a quilt, blankets and

88 *Late 15th-century timber frame, Welwyn rectory*

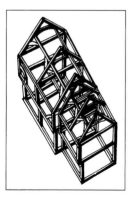

89 *The author's own house, left, despite its Georgian windows and brick noggin, gives some idea of the sort of house which a well-to-do medieval person could have built. The 15th-century old rectory, Welwyn.*

sheets. Among wills, loose upholstery and coverlets for furniture are often mentioned, and cushions were evidently considered important—a reflection on the seating of the time. The Great Bed of Ware is a particularly famous piece of furniture, featured in Shakespeare's *Twelfth Night*. A local rhyme says:

> At Ware was a bed of dimensions so wide,
> Four couples might cosily lie side by side
> And thus without touching each other, abide ...

According to tradition it was made by Jonas Fosbrooke, journeyman carpenter of Ware, for Edward IV and his guests, but modern experts date it to the late 16th century. After centuries in hotels in Ware—the *Crown*, the *Bull*, the *Saracen's Head*—it was exhibited in the late 19th century at Rye House. It is now in the Victoria and Albert Museum.

Close to London as it is, Hertfordshire has never been far from the centre of national events. In 1295 St Albans, which had seen the drafting of Magna Carta 80 years before, was the venue of the 'Model Parliament', to which every city, borough and main town sent two representatives or burgesses. Beset as he was by war and a defiant nobility, Edward I needed money, but more importantly, also consensus. 'What touches all should be approved of all,' ran the summons to the Model Parliament, 'and it is also clear that common dangers should be met by measures approved of in common.' In Hertfordshire, several towns claimed the right to send burgesses to Parliament, but these claims were disputed. St Albans made claims to borough status which, as we have seen, were denied by the abbey. The sheriffs made confused returns to the central government on the matter. In 1320, for example, Stortford, Berkhamsted

90 *Edward II, St Alb-ans Abbey*

91 *Brass of John Per-yent, 1415, Digswell*

and Hertford each sent two burgesses, and St Albans none. Six years later, Richard de Perrers, Sheriff of both Hertfordshire and Essex at the time, returned burgesses for Colchester only, declaring that there were no other boroughs within his bailiwick.

Royal visits to Hertfordshire were frequent throughout the Middle Ages: usually for pleasure but sometimes for grimmer reasons. Edward II frequently kept court at the royal palace of King's Langley and in 1308 bestowed the honour of Berkhamsted upon his favourite, Piers Gaveston. Edward's excessive favouring of Gaveston, and his failure to live up to the standards which his father had maintained in the administration and in military matters, aroused great discontent. In 1311 Gaveston's banishment was demanded, and when he ventured to return after only a short absence, the barons assembled at Dunstable, clearly demonstrating their opposition to royal policy. Gaveston was captured and executed at Scarborough, but his body was buried at King's Langley, with the Abbot of St Albans officiating. This act earned the abbey the king's favour, and it received lavish gifts from him.

After Edward's eventual deposition and death, Hertfordshire continued to enjoy royal favour. His widow Isabella spent much time at Berkhamsted and at Hertford, where she died in 1358, and her son Edward III frequently stayed at King's Langley with his Queen, Philippa of Hainault; their son Prince Edmund was born there in 1345. During Edward III's reign, the poet Geoffrey Chaucer was appointed Clerk of the Works at Berkhamsted and Langley, but there is no evidence that he actually visited Hertfordshire; the post was a sinecure and he appointed a subordinate to do the actual work involved. Later in the 14th century, Richard II, and his Lancastrian successors Henry IV and Henry V, all stayed at Langley; and the Tudor dynasty's long connection with the county may be said to have begun in 1430, when Edmund Tudor, Earl of Richmond and future father of Henry VII, was born at Hadham.

In 1455 St Albans was the scene of the first major engagement of the long and confusing struggle which was to become known as the Wars of the Roses. The forces of the Duke of York were camped on Key Field, to the west of the town (about where London Road station is today), and those of King Henry VI marched into the town barricading all the entrances after them. It appears that at this time there were no proper walls or gates, only a substantial encircling earthwork called Tonman's Ditch. A contemporary letter describes what happened next:

> The king, then being in the place of Edmund Westby, hundreder of the said town of St Albans, comaundeth to slay all manner men of lords, knights, esquires and yeomen that might be taken of the aforesaid Duke of York. This done, the ... Lord Clifford kept strongly the barriers that the said Duke of York might not, in any wise, with all the power that he had, enter, nor break into the town. The Earl of Warwick [who was fighting on York's side] knowing thereof, took and gathered his men together, and fiercely brake in by the garden sides, between the sign of the Key and the sign of the Chekkers in Holywell Street; and anon, they were in the town, and suddenly they blew up trumpets, and set a cry with a shout and a great voice, 'A Warwick, A Warwick!'

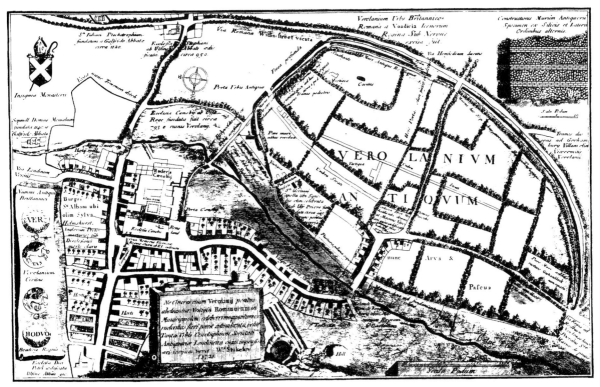

Warwick and his men crossed Tonman's Ditch, and quite literally smashed their way through the houses, into what is now Chequer Street, but was at that time still part of the great market place. The defenders at the barricades were thus attacked from the rear, and the fighting was over in half an hour. The streets were filled with the fallen and about fourteen hundred men were interred at St Peter's Church. The King was taken, according to tradition in a tanner's cottage, and was escorted to London the next day as a virtual prisoner.

In 1460 the war came to St Albans again. This time Warwick already had the king under his control, and camped on Bernards Heath, just north of the town, prepared to encounter the queen's forces coming from the north. The latter outmanoeuvred Warwick by a forced night march, and approached down Watling Street. In the city, they advanced up Fishpool Street, but found Church Lane (now George Street) blocked by a barricade. They were driven back by archers on the tops of surrounding buildings. They struck north along the line of Tonman Ditch and eventually broke in at Catherine Street. Most of the Yorkist army were defeated at Bernards Heath; the remainder were pursued to Nomansland and killed there. The queen's forces, however, abandoned themselves to pillaging the city and the surrounding countryside, losing the advantage they might have gained from an immediate march on London. Meanwhile the young Duke of York, Edward, who had inherited the quarrel from his father, marched to the capital and was crowned king as Edward IV.

92 'The Spencer interest derives from the manor of Holywell.' Stukeley's map of St Albans of 1721 shows 'Fons Sacer', the holy well from which the manor takes its name (centre left) as well as the Roman city of 'Verolamium'.

93 Oxford's Arms: the de Vere Star

A third important battle of the Wars of the Roses took place in Hertfordshire, at Barnet in 1471. The Earl of Warwick, now in opposition to Edward IV, was advancing on London and camped on Hadley Green, intending to encounter the royal forces in the narrow confines of the main street of Chipping Barnet. Edward, however, arrived at dusk and disposed his men under cover of darkness. The battle next day took place in the confusing conditions of a thick mist; it seems that the arms of Warwick's ally the Earl of Oxford, the de Vere Star, were mistaken in the bad light for the Yorkist rose, the Rose en Soleil, and the would-be allies fought each other. Afterwards Warwick was executed, and thereafter Edward's authority went largely unchallenged.

94   *The Yorkist Rose en Soleil*

8

Tudor and Stuart Hertfordshire

In 1555 two events occurred which were both to have profound future effects; Henry Manners, Earl of Rutland, had the first English coach built, and Parliament brought in legislation which made each individual parish responsible for the upkeep of the roads which passed through it. The parish appointed a Surveyor of Highways annually and parishioners had to give four (later six) days' unpaid labour, as well as providing materials, tools and carts. The surveyors were unqualified, untrained, and had little authority. The villagers resented having to give their labour for a task which benefited others—passing travellers—more than themselves, and generally treated the 'boon-days' as unpaid holidays and occasions for fun and frolic. It was not until 1639 that the surveyors were legally entitled to levy a rate to pay for road repair materials. Often a very small parish found itself responsible for a short stretch of a major road, but without sufficient labour and perhaps, due to geological factors, without suitable materials for its upkeep.

The development of the Great North Road was typical of many. The route that Sir Robert Carey took to Edinburgh in 1603 to tell King James of Scotland that he was now king of England as well was almost the same road that the Romans would have taken, with the exception that, south of Ware, the line of Ermine Street, which passed over London clay with no stone available for repairs, had been abandoned for the older valley route. This route was far from ideal: a diarist noted in 1695 that rain had 'raised the washes upon the roads near Ware to the hight that passengers from London that were upon the road swam, and a poor higgler [pedlar] was drowned'.

At least the river itself provided a main artery of communication to London. To the north, however, there was no alternative to the roads, along which much traffic, especially barley for malting carried by wagon and packhorse, converged on Ware, blocking the highway with slow-moving traffic and churning up the boulder clay into fearsome ruts. In 1639 a ban was placed on carts carrying more than one ton, or drawn by more than five horses. Small wonder that the 'polite' traffic should seek out an alternative route to the north more suited to wheeled vehicles. A moderately good road led from London to Hatfield, the site of a great house—indeed, a former royal palace. North of Welwyn ran the ill-maintained, but more or less direct, vestiges of the Roman road to Baldock.

95 *Sir Robert Carey*

*96 'New locks were
constructed at Hod-
desdon ... and the
minimum depth and width
of the navigation were
determined.'*

A winding cross-country route was cobbled together from pieces of the random network of roads in between. From Hatfield House the road ran to Stanborough and thence to Brocket Corner (where Lemsford Church now stands), before turning sharp right to plunge down to Lemsford Mill. Skirting the boundary of Brocket Park, it passed Ayot Green, went down a deep and waterlogged valley known as 'Mountain Slough' before dropping down a perilous slope into Welwyn. A sharp right turn at Welwyn Church brought travellers onto the old Roman road.

This twisting and ill-maintained route became known as the 'Great North Road' to distinguish it from the Ware route, the 'Old North Road'. A great road indeed; in 1723 the parishioners of Welwyn were presented at Quarter Sessions for failing to make the road eight feet wide! Although a national road policy was submitted to the Parliament of 1657, nothing was done. The idea of charging tolls to road users, and thus obtaining sufficient funds to keep them in adequate repairs, finally came to fruition only in 1663, and then only on a stretch of the Old North Road.

With such poor roads, the rivers naturally had great importance as freight-carriers. In 1571 an act of Parliament 'for bryngynge of ye River of Lee to ye Northside of Ye Citie of London' involved a new cut of over four and a quarter miles from Temple Mills to Moorgate 'to carry Merchandize, Victuals and Other Necessaries ... . And also for Tiltboats and Wherries for conveying the Queens subjects'. At this time, the river was scoured as far as Ware, but when six years later Thomas Fanshawe, Clerk of Ware, took a boat of 18-inch draught down the river, it touched bottom in several places, which was clearly not satisfactory. In 1580 an order from the queen to clean and repair probably resulted in the construction of the first pound lock at Waltham Abbey, described in 1589 as 'a rare devise ... . This locke contains two double doors of woode, within the same cisterne all of plankes which only fills when boates come there to passes by opening these mighty doores by sleight'. As the navigation improved, local carters found the competition crippling. They made cuts in the bank, broke bridges, drove sharpened stakes in the river bed, threatened bargemasters, and even tried to burn the lockgates. In 1594 they challenged the legality of the right-of-way enjoyed on the towpath; the bargees won the case.

97 *Roof of Hatfield Palace, 1497*

Despite the immense problems of transport, traditional Hertfordshire industries continued to flourish. References to maltsters crop up throughout the period, usually concerning their contravention of regulations, as when Isaac Fuller, late of Ware, used an illicit measure in 1640. In the reign of Charles I, an attempt was made by the central government to discourage Hertfordshire malting, since, according to a statement of 1636:

> The most maltsters in that county are of mean ability, and are chiefly employed by gentlemen and others who send their barleys to them to be malted for the provision of their houses; also widows, the portions of orphans, servants who have some small stock and others who like not to put their money to usury, buy barley and hire the making of it by the quarters. These poor maltsters are very useful to the county, pay rents and have borne all taxes. So in the villages many petty maltsters make malt for themselves, and supply the markets; they bear offices and pay taxes, but being restrained, must turn day-labourers, of whom many want work. So again malt-making continued little more than half a year; many mechanics and men of small trades employed their wives, children and servants in malt-making, whilst themselves followed other callings.

Allowing for the bias of this account, two points are noteworthy: the occupation was a seasonal one, and was looked upon as a short-term investment. The seasonal nature of the work was a result of the difficulties of controlling the conditions in a maltings during the summer, when, in any case, other agricultural work was available. In the investment of capital in the industry can be seen the first glimmerings of the process from which banking was eventually to grow.

98 *Queen Hoo, Tewin*

The addition of hops to ale wort to produce beer was probably first introduced into England in the 15th century, but the first Hertfordshire record refers to 'the Dutchman [who may have been a German] the bere bruer' at Ware in 1504. Ten years later a Welwyn innkeeper was described as 'retaliator de la bere'. By the late 16th century, an Order in Council instructed that alehouse keepers 'shall not brew in their own houses, but take drink from their brewer', a clear indication that brewing was becoming an industry. Home brewing, however, continued, if on an ever-decreasing scale. It was probably the improvement in the storage life of beer which permitted brewing to become a major industry in the 18th century, when there were some fifty breweries in the county. Brewers and maltsters diversified, investing in their own barges for use on the Lea, which carried malt to London, and in their own retail outlets, developing the 'tied house' system.

Although the county was never outstanding for wool production, frequent references to fulling mills and fullers indicate that there was a significant amount of cloth manufacture. There were weavers and dyers in Ware, Hertford and St Albans in the 13th century, and in the later 14th century in one year the equivalent of 198 cloths were produced (4,500 yards by one and three-quarter yards) at St Albans, Hertford, Berkhamsted, Ashwell and Hitchin. There seems to have been a gradual decline in the industry, however, and when in 1588 the St Albans authorities wanted to set the unemployed to spinning and weaving, they employed a German, who brought over his equipment from Hertford:

> A new great loom and two flayles, one for silk and the other for cruell, and all the things that belongs to them ... two little looms, one for silk and one for cruell ... seven wheels ... wheels to wind yarn ... three blades ... things to lay on the warp ... the warping pins belonging to them and four dozen quills ... one hartle ... two keeles ... a pair of combes ... .

Mention has been made of dyers. Woad was the common dyestuff of the English wool trade. It was imported in large quantities, but from the late 16th century it was grown in this country, often on freshly-cleared ground. In 1606 the inhabitants of Stansted Abbots were greatly annoyed by 'the making of wode' which made passers-by 'constrained to stop their nosses as they go bye, the stinke is so great'. (A writer of 1823 informs us that woad is in a proper condition for the dyer's use when there is a change of smell, 'from one which is most putrid, and offensive, to one which is more agreeable and sweet'.)

One unusual industry related to the manufacture of clothing was to be found in Hertfordshire: this was the manufacture of straw hats. It was not, however, thought remarkable by contemporaries, and so its beginnings are not documented. In 1530 an immigrant from Guelderland was described as a 'strawen ... hatmaker'. At the beginning of the 17th century, however, there was a great growth in the industry, based on the Chilterns area of Bedfordshire, Buckinghamshire and Hertfordshire. In 1667 Pepys noted the pleasure which the ladies of his party, on a visit to Hatfield, took in 'putting on some straw hats which are much worn in this country, and did become them mightily, especially my wife'. The size of the straw hat industry can be gauged from the reaction to a bill of 1689 which contained a clause to encourage the wearing of woollen hats. It was protested that this would threaten the livelihood of 'fourteen

99 *19th-century straw bonnet*

thousand persons at the least' who were employed in the Chilterns manufacturing straw hats.

Straw hats were not woven like baskets, but were made by sewing
together continuous flat braids or 'twists' in an overlapping spiral. The
twists were plaited by hand. The type of straw required was thin-walled
wheat straw, free from disease, with at least nine inches between the
nodes. The best straw usually came from the worst land, and was care-
fully cut by hand. It was sometimes bleached, using burning brimstone.

Another group of traditional industries was based on the exploita-
tion of the county's woodlands. Even today, most Hertfordshire woodland is still recognisably coppice, in which the 'pole wood' was periodically felled, leaving the stumps to regenerate into a further crop of poles.
Hedges were another important source of timber, and many trees in
hedges, or standing in meadows, have the characteristic shape produced
by pollarding. In the 16th century there was a near-disastrous exploita-
tion of woodland. There was a great increase in house-building, and
carpenters turned to the use of straight sawn timber, a practice wasteful
of wood. In addition, the new owners of monastic lands, heedless of the
future, often clear-felled the timber and thus used up assets which they
did not replace.

Royal authority extended only over woodland owned by the Crown,
and it became clear that destruction was widespread. The preamble to an
act of 1543 which laid down rules for the management of woodland,
stated that:

> There is great and manifest likelihood of scarcity and lack as well of timber for
> building, making, repairing and maintaining of houses and ships, and also of fewel
> and fire-wood for the necessary relief of the whole commonality of this ... realme.

The reign of Elizabeth saw the appointment of a number of commissions concerned with the maintenance of Hertfordshire woodlands, as in
1575, when they were concerned with the damage to woods at Colney
Heath, and in 1591 when woods formerly belonging to the priory of
Dunstable were investigated.

Charcoal was (and to a very small extent, still is) burnt in the woods
for local consumption and for carriage to London. The scale of the trade
in the past can be judged by the fact that in 1475 the manor of Bedwell
sold 62 cartloads.

Not all trees were grown for purely economic reasons. Many gentle-
men maintained the trees in their parks from aesthetic motives: Cassiobury
Park was justifiably famous. The work here was carried out by Moses
Cook, whose book *The Manner of Raising, Ordering and Improving
Forest Trees* contained an effusive dedication to Arthur Capel, Earl of
Essex:

100 *A coppice 'stool'*

> To your eternal praise be it spoken that there is many a fine tree which you have
> nursed from seeds sown by your own hands, and many thousands more which you
> have commanded me to raise ... . The large plantation you have made will abundantly
> testify your ability and promptitude in promoting the planting and improving of
> forest trees.

101 *Sir Nicholas Bacon*

Reference has already been made to the great increase in building during this period, partly encouraged by the sudden availability of new lands—and of materials—from the dissolved religious houses. Examples of new houses built on former religious sites include Sir Humphrey Bouchier's Markyate and Sir Anthony Denny's fine house at Cheshunt. One notable newcomer to county society was Ralph Rowlatt, goldsmith, banker, and merchant of the Staple of Calais, who bought much of the property of St Albans Abbey. At one point he owned Gorhambury, The Pre, Westwick, Sandridge, Napsbury, Michenbury, Barley, Codicote, Newnham and Radlett, as well as the advowsons (right of presentation of incumbents) of many of the churches.

The 16th century saw the disappearance or radical alteration of many medieval castles. Berkhamsted Castle was disused, and its demolition to provide building materials for local houses began in 1580. By 1603 much of Hertford Castle had been levelled to the ground. Langley Palace was not used by royalty after 1538, and was sold by Charles I; the park returned to agricultural use in 1627.

It might seem that brick was an obvious choice of building material for a county which had no hard freestone but, curiously enough, the earliest post-Roman brick structures in Hertfordshire, both gate-houses, date as late as 1443 (Rye House) and 1461 (Hertford Castle). John Morton, Archbishop of Canterbury under Henry VII, built one of our first brick palaces at Hatfield, between 1480 and 1490, and Knebworth was built in 1492. Of Morton's Hatfield, only the hall remains. The rest was replaced by one of the most important Jacobean mansions in England. Both Theobalds and Cassiobury, vast palatial mansions which entertained Queen Elizabeth on her visits to the county, have vanished, and the Gorhambury of Sir Nicholas Bacon, one of Elizabeth's most trusted servants, survives only as a ruin in the grounds of the 18th-century mansion which succeeded it.

102 *'The earliest post-Roman brick structures in Hertfordshire ... date as late as 1443.' The surviving part, the gateway, of Rye House, near Hoddesdon.*

Mention of these great houses is sufficient indication that Hertfordshire saw as many royal visitors in the Tudor period as it had in the centuries before. Henry VIII frequently came to the county to hunt and hawk: legend has it that he nearly drowned whilst hawking near Wymondley, when a pole broke as he was vaulting a ditch. He was at Hertford Castle in 1528 in the company of his wife Queen Catherine and her maids, including Anne Boleyn, when there was an outbreak of sweating sickness. The visitors fled, the royal couple to Hunsdon and Anne home to Kent. Here she fell ill with the sickness, and was the recipient of passionate letters of sympathy and love from the king. While the divorce of Catherine and Henry was being discussed, the Queen stayed at Cardinal Wolsey's palace, The More, another early brick building which has since disappeared. It is a local tradition that the secret marriage of Henry and Anne Boleyn took place at Sopwell.

Deprived of her household and her titles, declared illegitimate, Catherine's daughter Mary lived as maid-in-waiting to her infant half sister Elizabeth at Hatfield, a virtual prisoner. Following Anne's execution, both princesses were declared illegitimate and lived together at Hunsdon. Their brother Edward spent much of his childhood at Ashridge, and Elizabeth returned to Hatfield during the reigns of both Edward and Mary. It was here, on 17 November 1558, that Sir Nicholas Throckmorton brought her the news that Mary was dead, and that she was queen of England. Her first Privy Council was held in 'the greate halle' of Hatfield Palace.

103   *Henry VIII*

Elizabeth's successor, King James I, was entertained by Robert Chester at Royston on his way to London for his coronation. It is obvious that he was immediately taken with Hertfordshire. He rented Chester's house while two nearby inns were converted into a royal hunting lodge, and four years later exchanged his palace of Hatfield with that of Robert Cecil at Theobalds. He continued to spend much time at Royston, which led to a great deal of attention being paid to the maintenance of local roads and bridges. However, local people considered that the disadvantages of royal favour outweighed the benefits. Their agricultural pursuits were severely limited by the needs of the royal hunt: fences were taken down; ridge and furrow ploughing, which might pose problems for galloping horses, was forbidden; and pigs had to have rings in their noses to stop them rooting out acorns and making holes which might trip riders. On one occasion, the locals found an original way of petitioning the king, when one of the royal hunting dogs, named Jowler, came home with a note tied to its collar:

104   *King James I ... continued to spend much time at Royston. Although the shell canopied door and the venetian window are 18th-century insertions, this 'palace' at Royston was part of James' favourite* pied-à-terre.

> Good Mr. Jowler, we pray you to speak to the King (for he hears you every day and so he doth not us) that it will please His Majesty to go back to London, for else the country will be undone; all our provision is spent already and we are not able to entertain him longer.

Despite this eloquent plea, James was still hunting, shooting and hawking at Royston shortly before his death in 1625.

Elizabeth I had frequently been a visitor to Sir Nicholas Bacon at Gorhambury, and for a short time in James's reign the

house regained its former importance at the centre of state affairs, when Sir Nicholas's son, Sir Francis Bacon, became Lord Chancellor. In 1622, however, he was charged with bribery and corruption and lost his post and influence in consequence. His lasting fame, however, rests on his philosophical writings, which made a major contribution to the development of post-medieval thought.

The comings and goings of royalty, however, had little impact on the daily life of most Hertfordshire folk, apart from the longsuffering inhabitants of Royston. Awareness of themselves as Englishmen, of any loyalty larger than the parish or perhaps the county, was still slight. The parish was still the principal administrative unit through which legislation was put into practice—for the repair of roads, for instance, as we have already seen, or for the maintenance of the poor. Thus the vestry or parish council took over the functions of the old manorial courts. In Welwyn, for example, the

105 *The Gorhambury of Sir Nicholas Bacon, one of Elizabeth's most trusted servants, survives as a ruin in the grounds of the 18th-century mansion which succeeded it.*

106 *Edward VI*

last records for the appointment of constables by each of the two manors with property in the parish were in 1632 and 1636. Thereafter the constables were appointed by the parish council.

A constable's duties were wide-ranging, He was not just the keeper of the peace and the punisher of transgressors, but also the local trading standards officer and surveyor. He was expected to 'take before the Justices those who sleep by day and walk by night, or haunt bawdy houses' and to arrest 'strange persons abroad in the night season, those carrying weapons ... those who threaten to kill or use hot words, who make rumour or assembly of people, make affray, those not attending church, profane swearers ... popish recusants' as well as those 'who be in fornication or adulteries together'. At the same time he had to make presentments of the state of roads and bridges, of provisions for the poor, instruments of punishment, weights and measures and those local residents balloted for militia service. No pay was available, although the constable could claim expenses. However, until the 1835 Poor Law Act, it seems that many constables received an official salary taken out of the

IX *The Garden of St Pauls Walden Bury. This format of alleys aligned on statues and other features was originally designed by Edward Gilbert in 1730. Her Majesty the Queen and her sister played here as children.*

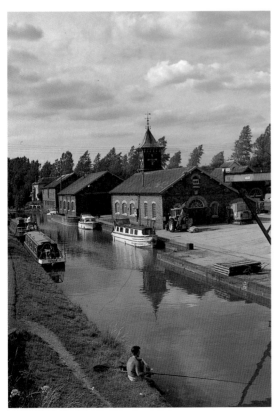

X *The architecture of the canal age is clearly shown in this picture of the Grand Union Canal at Bulbourne near Tring.*

XI *Berkhamsted by George Sidney Shepherd*

XII *Queen Hoo, Tewin. An impressive Elizabethan brick hunting lodge, set in a tangled Saxon landscape.*

poor rate, the tax levied on well-
to-do parishioners for the upkeep
of their poorer neighbours. If the
constable asked too much of the
parishioners, they sometimes re-
elected him as a punishment!

The accounts of a constable
in Baldock during the late 17th
century have survived, and give a
vivid picture of his work. Included
are rates levied for quarterage
(expenses in connection with attendance at the quarter sessions);
robbery money (a communal fine
levied when a crime remained
unsolved); bridge money (towards
repairs); town armour (for arms
and armour); light and fuel for the
guard (who kept watch at night);
and for passing vagrants. Reports
on licensing, jury lists and militia
rolls are also preserved. Watchmen
often ran into danger from wrong-
doers they detected in action, like
those at Barkway in June 1606,
who tried to arrest a man called
Thomas Hunte:

> He the withinbounde Thomas Hunte
> upon the 29th day of June last past
> and in the night tyme, after the watch
> was sett and charged in the town of
> Barkwaye within named, behaved
> himselve   verye   unlawfullye,
> unpeaceablye and disorderlye in the
> same town and against Michael
> Toppen, Christopher Fordham, John
> Game and Henry Numan, watchmen
> appoynted for that night and did at
> that tyme threaten afterwardes to kill
> or wounde them ...

The practice had grown up, time out of mind, of 'moving on' a
vagabond or stranger who might become a burden on the parish. In 1622
the constable of Welwyn was presented to quarter sessions because he
had allowed 'divers vagabonds and strangers to loiter' in the parish, and
in 1624 the constables of the hundreds of Hertfordshire were ordered to
instigate 'a privy search for rogues and vagabonds' every fortnight. In
one month in 1639 the constables of Barnet reported that they had
'whippt and past' eight men and three women on to other places. The

107 *'His lasting fame ...
rests on his philosophical
writings, which made a
major contribution to
post-medieval thought.'
The pensive effigy of Sir
Francis Bacon in St
Michael's Church, St
Albans.*

108 *The lockup at Shenley*

infamous Act of Settlement and Removal in 1662, which required that a newcomer who did not inhabit property of the annual rental value of £10 (a sum quite beyond the resources of a labourer or even a craftsman) was to be returned to his place of settlement within 40 days, was thus only giving clear definition to a state of affairs which had long existed. This policy did nothing to solve the problem of vagrancy, and it was costly to administer.

Poverty was seen as a national problem needing statutory action in the 16th century, and as early as 1535 an act was passed prohibiting begging and the distribution of indiscriminate charity. However, it failed to set up any system for alleviating the situation. A series of acts in the early 17th century required 'overseers of the poor' to collect a tax from well-to-do parishioners to feed and house the poor, and to set the able-bodied paupers tos work. 'Houses of correction' were set up 'for the punishing and setting to work of rogues, vagabonds and other idle persons'; there were eight in Hertfordshire. The nature of these establishments can be judged from the fittings of the one at Hitchin, which included a 'block to knock hemp on' and a whipping post.

As the eventual destination of an expelled vagrant was his 'home' house of correction or 'bridewell', so called after the notorious establishment in London, it is clear that these were places of incarceration and punishment. The following instruction to the keeper of the Hertford bridewell gives us some idea of the kind of treatment meted out to vagrants:

> Whereas Marie Armstrong, an idle, lewde, vagrant beggar, was this 24th day June 1675 by Arthur Younge of Kempton, Constable there and George Williams, husbandman, brought before me, Edward Wingate, Esq., ... and charged as well with begging and idle wandering abroad, and also with other lewde and disorderly behaviour so she appears to be dangerous to the people as one who has not reformed her roguish life. These are therefore to will and require you to receive the said Marie Armstrong and her safely keepe in your said house [the bridewell] until the next Quarter Sessions, and during that time she shall so continue with you, you hold her to work and labour and punish her by putting fetters and gyves on her, and by moderate whipping of her as in good discretion you shall find cause.

Gaols too were terrible places. There were two in the county, one in the gatehouse of St Albans Abbey, and one in Hertford. One must sympathise with Jonathan Rose, who in 1692 had been imprisoned at Hertford for ten months 'when he might have been cleared on condition he enlist'. He petitioned the quarter sessions 'to be allowed to join the Earl of Derby's regiment of dragoons' rather than being again remanded in custody.

109 *A Hertfordshire work-house*

Independently of the houses of correction and the gaols, many parishes provided for their poor by boarding them out, and by almshouses, founded by charitable persons to house the poor sick or incapable. By the end of the 16th century, many of these provided profitable ways for the poor to be employed, in contrast to the brutal treatment meted out in the bridewells. In 1618 Stephen Langley proposed to teach methods of weaving 'curious woollens and excellent yarns' at the St Albans almshouse

110 *'At the end of 1539, Richard Boreman, the abbot of St Albans, surrendered the abbey to the king.' The great gateway of the abbey dates from the 1360s. It has served as a prison.*

and in 1630 at Hitchin Jeremiah Hockley taught 'the mystery of flax-dressing, the spinning of linen and the making of straw hats'.

In theory, every able-bodied Englishman was expected to render military service to his king and country in time of war, and the training necessary for this purpose was provided, like so much else, at parish level. In practice, militia service could be neglected and even avoided altogether by those who could afford to buy themselves immunity from it. Nevertheless, Hertfordshire was especially commended for the efficiency of its fighting men during Queen Elizabeth's reign. Hertfordshire soldiers served in campaigns in France and Holland, as well as rendering service in the queen's bodyguard. When mobilised in 1588 for the expected invasion by the Spanish, the county sent 25 lances and 60 light horse to Brentwood, 1,000 foot soldiers to Tilbury, another 1,000 to Stratford-at-Bow, and 500 men to guard Her Majesty's own person.

In 1640, the Hertfordshire trained bands recalled in a petition to Parliament their loyal service to Elizabeth at the time of the Armada. They declined to serve either under strange officers or abroad, and, turning from their specific grievances to those of opponents of the government in general, complained that since:

> this Church and Kingdome being by prelates, those multitudes of corrupt and scandalous Ministers (their Creatures) and the Popish party concurring with them on one hand; and by wicked Councellors: evil Ministers of State, and great swarms of Projectors and others ill affected to the peace of this Realme, on the other, brought to a sad and almost desperate condition, and thereby the splendour of His Majesty's Crown and dignity [was] dangerously weakened and eclipsed.

111 *The arms of Hert-fordshire, a rebus (her-aldic pun), granted 1589*

Parliament was 'the only means (under God) to reforme the many pres-sures and grievances of the Church and Kingdome, and to remove the causes thereof'.

It is not surprising, therefore, to find that the county was predomi-nantly in support of the Parliamentarian cause when civil war broke out two years later. However, the king's own standard bearer, Sir Edmund Verney, who was killed in the first battle of the war at Edgehill, came from Pendley, and gentlemen from Hertfordshire were to be found in both armies. Families were indeed often divided amongst themselves: Thomas Tookes was a Royalist, but his two sons were Parliamentarians.

The county's geographical position brought it much suffering during the war. Armies stopped here in transit, or camped in idleness, at a convenient distance from the capital, awaiting further orders. Dispersed and mutinous bands of deserters roamed and pillaged at will. St Albans was particularly noted as a Parliamentary stronghold, and the Earl of Essex, Parliament's leading general for much of the early part of the war, often used it as his headquarters. Despite this, in January 1643 the sheriff, Sir Thomas Coningsby, had the temerity to read a proclamation to mobilise the militia for the king. He was interrupted by a troop of horsemen and taken prisoner. The leader of the troop was Oliver Cromwell.

Both Parliamentary and Royalist troops ravaged the Chilterns. Troops plundered Ashridge, and killed deer in the park. Little Gaddesden Church was rifled, and the tombs broken open. One of the worst pe-riods for the county was the winter of 1643-4, when the Parliamentary army, unpaid and ill-provisioned, wintered at St Albans before moving down to the West Country. Another frightening episode took place in 1645, when Cromwell's New Model Army committed outrages against the local population and their property; 12 of them were hanged for their crimes.

In 1647 the war was, in theory, over; but Parliament, which had created the army, could now neither afford to pay the soldiers their arrears, nor persuade them to disband without them. The soldiers held a 'parliament' of their own on Thriploe Heath, near Royston, and sent a letter to London, calling for the pay owed to 2,000 men and for a purge of the Parliament which they felt had betrayed them. By Novem-ber, Cromwell and Sir Thomas Fairfax, the army's two most senior commanders, were maintaining their authority over their rebellious men only with difficulty. Not only were the soldiers demanding their back-pay; many of them were also affected by the ideas of the Levellers, a political faction which sought to introduce a greater measure of demo-cracy into the 'constitutional structure of the country. The army and its officers, who generally, as gentlemen of property themselves, had little sympathy with the Levellers, debated these ideas, but eventually Cromwell decided the only way to regain control was by force. At Cockbush Field, Ware, he confronted the 'agitators' who were respon-sible for spreading Leveller pamphlets to the soldiers, and took them

112 *Queen Elizabeth I*

prisoner. A number of them were sentenced to death, but eventually as an act of 'mercy' only one was actually shot, the victim being selected by lot.

The split in the ranks of those who had fought for Parliament was now impossible to close. The army leaders, having regained control over their own soldiers, tried and failed to make Parliament agree to pay the arrears, and to promise to bring the king himself, whom officers and soldiers alike regarded as the principal agent of the war, to trial. In December 1648 Cromwell's trusted subordinate Colonel Pride stood at the doors of the House of Commons with a troop of soldiers and arrested all those M.P.s who were unsympathetic to the army's views. The remaining M.P.s, known as the 'Rump Parliament', were willing to co-operate, either from ideological motives, or for simple reasons of self preservation. In January 1649 Charles I, after a public trial, was executed. The army, which had received at least some of its pay at long last, was dealt with by being sent north to Scotland in pursuit of the young Charles II, and later to crush rebels in Ireland. It was not too soon for Hertfordshire, where the demands of the soldiers had greatly aggravated the problems caused by crop failure after a disastrously wet summer.

113   *Francis Bacon*

The Civil War and the rule of the Commonwealth and Cromwell's Protectorate which followed brought much hardship to supporters of the Royalist cause. Gentlemen's estates were confiscated unless they could show proof of active support of Parliament, and only restored on payment of steep fines. These gentlemen were also, of course, excluded from serving in Parliament or from any kind of office holding.

With the restoration of Charles II to the throne in 1660, the situation was reversed. Confiscated estates, some of which had actually been taken over by supporters of Parliament, were in some cases restored to their original owners; a new, aggressively Royalist, Parliament was elected; and many office-holders lost their profitable posts. Opposition to 'popery' and fond memories of the past remained in the minds of those who had supported Parliament.

There was fierce opposition to the nomination of Charles II's brother, James, as his heir, mainly on religious grounds, as James was a Catholic. A number of plots were afoot, one of which, in 1683, it was said involved a plan to assassinate both the King and his brother as they rode back to London from Newmarket, the attempt to be at Rye House in Hertfordshire. One of the alleged protagonists was a maltster, Richard Rumbold, who was a fanatically republican survivor of Cromwell's army, and was the tenant of The Rye at the time. The plot was foiled by the early return of the royal party. Its discovery was used as an excuse for a purge of all the Whig leaders. Essex was taken at Cassiobury, and committed suicide in the Tower, and others were executed. Rumbold escaped to France, but came over to Scotland shortly afterwards. He was taken and 'one part of his quartered body' was displayed on his maltings.

At the time of the Monmouth Rebellion in 1685, when Charles II's illegitimate but Protestant son, the Duke of Monmouth, attempted to claim the throne from James II, it is clear that there was a considerable amount of sympathy with his cause in Hertfordshire. Many were bound over and had to give securities to keep the peace, and others were brought up before the quarter sessions as 'disaffected to the government'. One Owen Love was committed to prison for inciting people to rise for Monmouth and John Etheridge was stated to have said that 'where the King has one on his side the Duke of Monmouth has thirty and where the said King's health is drunk once, the Duke's was drunk tenne times'.

114   *Robert Cecil*

9

Canals and Turnpikes

The canal age proper opened in 1761, with the construction of the Duke of Bridgewater's canal at Worsley near Manchester, and in a very few years the advantages of artificial waterways over roads for freight traffic became obvious. The towns of the Black Country were soon linked by canals, and by 1790 it was possible to send goods to London from Birmingham through the Oxford Canal and the Thames. In 1792 a route was surveyed for the Grand Junction Canel to join the Oxford Canal at Braunstone with the Thames at Brentford, cutting the journey by 84 miles. The first stretch (from Brentford to Uxbridge) was opened the same year. According to a local paper:

> The opening of this part of the canal was celebrated by a variety of mercantile persons of Brentford, Uxbridge and Rickmansworth and their vicinities, forming a large party, attended by a band of music, with flags and streamers and several pieces of cannon, in a pleasure boat belonging to the Corporation of the City of London, preceding several barges laden with timber, coals and other merchandise to Uxbridge.

The route was originally intended to go through a tunnel at Langleybury, but the Earls of Essex and Clarendon agreed to a route through their parks at Grove Park and Cassiobury, in return for large sums in compensation and the landscaping of the canal. It was extended as far as King's Langley in September, and to Hemel Hempstead in December 1797. In 1798 it reached Berkhamsted, and in 1799 Tring Summit. By 1800 a through-route to Braunston (and hence to Birmingham) was available, although part of it was by horse-drawn railway at Blisworth.

115 *Canal barge*

The Tring Summit Level is a massive cutting, high on the Chilterns, where a water supply was bound to be a problem. Each vessel crossing the top took with it 100,000 gallons of water into the locks at either end. A number of streams and springs were pressed into service, and reservoirs were constructed at Wilstone, Marworth and Startopsend. These were connected with one another, and with the canal, by paddles and steam pumps.

As might be expected, the canal company ran into trouble with other water users, especially millers. Where the canal linked with both the Gade and the Bulbourne, at Hemel Hempstead, the millers claimed over £4,000 in compensation for losses over seven months, despite the

116 *Cow Roast Lock, Grand Union Canal at 382 feet above sea level*

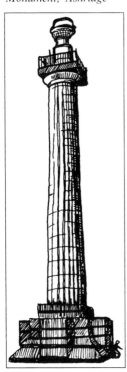

117 *The Bridgewater Monument, Ashridge*

installation of a steam engine to pump water back to the top of the locks. In 1852 millers brought an injunction preventing water being pumped from a well at Cow Roast, on the grounds that it would exhaust the supply and cause streams to dry up. A few years later, however, we find that the tables were turned, and the well actually supplied water during a drought, permitting mills to work when they would otherwise have been idle. The injunction was conveniently forgotten by both parties.

Other wrangles and difficulties also make interesting reading, since they throw light on the attitudes of the day. The Earl of Clarendon in 1811 objected to the use on Sundays of the canal which ran through his grounds. As a compromise, the company instructed its lock-keepers to allow no traffic to pass during the hours of Divine Service, whereupon the neighbouring landowner objected to what the bargees might be up to during their enforced idleness. The company gave a large donation to charity, and business was resumed as before.

Problems also arose over the purchase of land. At Boxmoor Common negotiations were made between the Company and representatives of the commoners; a price was agreed, and the canal was built. However, clearly the legality of this transaction was in some doubt, and wrangling continued until the Trustees of Boxmoor Common were appointed by Act of Parliament in 1809; their first action was to agree retrospectively that the sale of the land had been perfectly proper. In 1838 at Rickmansworth, a Mr. Dimes, then lord of the manor, discovered that the tenant of a piece of land, over which both the canal and a turnpike road passed, had died, and that, as copyhold land, in the absence of an heir the property reverted to the manor. He obstructed the passage of both the road and the canal on the grounds that he had not given leave for either, claiming £5,000 in compensation. While this claim was proceeding through the courts, the canal company traced the legitimate heir to the tenancy, whom Dimes was forced to accept on payment of a £1,500 fine for his absence—a fine which the company paid on the tenant's behalf with alacrity.

In 1926 the canal became known as the Grand Union Canal. Despite its initial problems, the canal was a success, and brought the Industrial Revolution to western Hertfordshire. It was not, of course, the only artery of water transport in the county. In 1766 the River Lea Act authorised the construction of cuts, locks and so forth on the river, and this was the start of a programme of continuous improvement of the Lea Navigation. The tonnage which could be conveyed on it, and the levels to be maintained, were fixed by further parliamentary acts in 1799 and 1805. Fifty years later new locks were constructed at Hoddesdon, Carthagena and Waltham Marsh, and the minimum depth and width of the navigation were determined.

Although goods of all kinds were carried, probably the most significant impact of the Lea Navigation was upon the malting industry. In the 18th century 5,000 quarters (1,500 cubic metres) of malt and corn a week were being carried. On return journeys, refuse and manure were conveyed out of London, and the latter used to increase soil fertility.

An earlier construction in the Lea valley was the aqueduct, first begun by Sir Hugh Middleton in 1609, to carry unpolluted water from Amwell spring to Stoke Newington (a distance of about twenty miles) and thence to London. At the beginning of the 19th century the spring was found to run dry in dry weather, and supplementary water is now taken from the Lea at King's Mead, between Hertford and Ware, via an ingenious metering device.

While the quantity of freight traffic carried was being increased by the use of canals, the lot of the traveller on the roads was also being improved. As late as 1725, Daniel Defoe could write of the Great North Road:

> This indeed is a most frightful way if we take it from Hatfield, or rather the park corners of Hatfield House, and from thence to Stevenage to Baldock, to Biggleswade and Bugden [Buckden]. Here is that famous lane called Baldock Lane [Radwell?] famous for being so impassable that coaches and travellers were obliged to break out of the way even by force, which the people of the country not able to prevent at length placed gates and laid their lands open, setting men at the gates to take voluntary toll which travellers always chose to pay rather than plunge into sloughs and holes that no horse could wade through.

He added that

> this terrible road is now under cure ... and probably may in time be bought firm and solid, the chalk and stones being not so far to fetch here.

118 'An early construction in the Lea valley was the aqueduct, first begun by Sir Hugh Middleton in 1609, to carry unpolluted water from Amwell spring ... to London.' This monument was erected at the source which supplied the New River.

In 1765, however many people in Woolmer Green, on the Great North Road, preferred to have their children baptised in Datchworth, rather than face the journey to the parish church at Welwyn, two miles south.

From the time of Elizabeth I parishes were responsible for the upkeep of main roads which ran through them, but this meant a patchy or neglected programme of upkeep, with little or no co-ordination. Radwell, one of the smallest parishes in the county, with a very small population, was responsible for the maintenance the Great Northern Road, and was entirely on gault clay, with no stone available. It could well have been

119 *'The only people prior to modern times actually to construct roads were the Roman engineers.' Ermine Street, south of Royston.*

the inspiration for Bunyan's 'Slough of Despond'.

Although the idea of a national road policy was put before Parliament in 1657, nothing was done. The idea of charging tolls to road users finally came to fruition in 1663, but then only on a short stretch of the road which included Radwell. The justices of three counties were authorised by an Act of Parliament to collect tolls at Wadesmill (Hertfordshire), Caxton (Cambridgeshire), and Stilton (Huntingdonshire). The preamble to the act referred to 'the great many loads that are weekly drawn in waggons and the great trade in malt that cometh to Ware' and described the road as being 'dangerous to all His Majesty's liege people that go that way'.

Opposition to the scheme was so strong that the toll-house at Stilton was not even built; that at Caxton was so easily by-passed that it was ineffective; and thus the first successful one in the countrywas at Wadesmill. The act failed to specify that a toll-gate should be erected and it is said none was provided. The first reference to a turnpike (meaning a gate) on a main road does not occur until forty years later.

At the beginning of the 18th century, Parliament began to appoint turnpike trusts, which consisted of local gentry, clergy and businessmen empowered to take control of specific stretches of road. In return for bringing roads up to an acceptable standard, and maintaining them thereafter, the trustees could charge tolls, intended to be sufficient both to pay for further upkeep, and to leave the trustees themselves with a profit. Turnpike finances were generally confused and trusts sometimes collapsed altogether: it was not until 1822 that trustees were required to produce their accounts for inspection.

The programme of turnpiking in Hertfordshire was haphazard. As an example, it took 18 years before the whole of that part of the Great North Road which ran through the county was turnpiked; however,

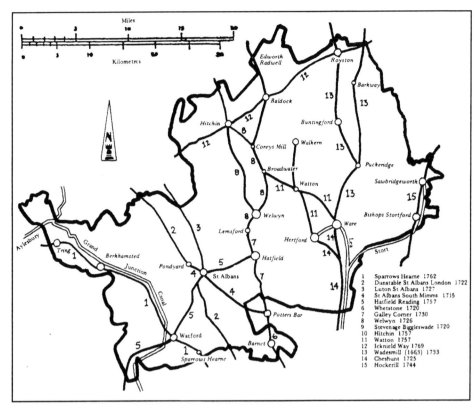

120 *John Tradescant, the gardener; carving on the staircase, Hatfield House*

121 *Turnpikes (with their dates of construction) and canals.*

future historians may compare this favourably with the improvements currently in progress along the A1! The road was turnpiked from Barnet to Potters Bar, and from Stevenage to Biggleswade by 1720. By 1726 the road from Lemsford Mill to Stevenage was taken under control by a trust.

As the roads and the design of coaches improved journey times were shortened and the number of travellers increased. An extract from the accounts of the St Albans Trust for the year June 1808-June 1809 gives some idea of the extent of the traffic on 11 miles of one road:

122 *Milestone on the 'Gout Track'*

Coaches etc. with six horses - 432
Coaches etc. with four horses - 10,883
Coaches etc. with three horses - 21
Chaises with two horses - 6,058
Waggons with five horses or more - 6,153
Waggons with four horses - 4,620
Carts with three horses or more - 1,830
Carts with two horses or less - 10,784
Horses - 22,262
Oxen - 71,249
Calves, hogs, sheep, lambs - 195,083

At about this time, the *White Hart*, the largest of the three coaching inns in Welwyn, was said to supply 'upwards of eighty stage coach teams of

123 *The railways effec-tively killed the coaching trade. There was a brief revival of a service from Hitchin to London in the 1880s when this picture was taken.*

horses daily'; if this is not an exaggeration, and the horses were literally supplied as teams, it would imply about 24,000 coaches passing through a year.

Tolls increased steadily throughout the history of the turnpikes. The charges for wagons often depended upon the width of the wheels and the weight, since narrow-wheeled heavily-loaded vehicles would do the most damage to the road. Charges for overloading were often prohibitive.

Highway robbery was still a problem, as it had been for centuries. 'Captain' James Whitney and 'Redbeard', both of whom roamed the Great North Road, have become unjustifiably confused with Dick Turpin. Toll collectors, often sited in isolated spots, were a frequent target for robbers. The Sparrows Herne Trust resolved on 22 November 1822 that:

> The thanks of this meeting be given to the Reverend Charles Lacy and the other inhabitants of Tring for their prompt exertions, which led to the immediate apprehension

of Thomas Randale, and James Croker, this day committed to the Gaol at Aylesbury on Suspicion of the Murder on Tuesday Night last of Edward Needle, the Toll Collector, and Rebecca his Wife at the Weston Turnpike Gate ...

The trust also arranged to pay the expenses both of the funeral and of the prosecution of the suspects. For real highway robbery, however, one would have difficulty in bettering the expedient adopted by one Joshua Cass, who in 1675 erected and maintained his own illegal 'turn picke' upon Amwell bridge!

Often parallel or complementary to the turnpike roads, one can trace other roads, often only 'macadamised' or 'made up' recently, if at all. These were probably used to evade the payment of tolls, but would have been useless for wheeled vehicles, and generally avoided towns. These were the drove roads. Apart from toll evasion, it must have been in the interests of all road users to keep the large herds of animals involved in droving off the main routes and the best road surfaces. One such route came down the Mimram Valley road to Welwyn, then, prior to its improvement, followed the route of the Great North Road up Mountain Slough, through Lemsford, and then skirted round Hatfield by the significantly-named 'Green', 'Travellers' and 'Bull' Lanes, joining 'the way from Hertford to London through the Green Lanes' by Potters Bar. In 1766, 992,400 beef cattle (including about 100,000 from Scotland) were driven to Smithfield market, many of them through Hertfordshire.

124 *'The* White Hart, *the largest of the three coaching inns in Welwyn, was able to supply "upwards of eighty stage coach teams of horses daily." In the 18th century the original timber-framed house was given a new brick front, and the Courthouse with banqueting chamber above was built to the right of the coaching entrance.*

The turnpike trusts repaired, re-routed and straightened roads, but improvement to the road surface did not come until the early years of the 19th century, mainly as a result of the work of John Loudon McAdam and his son James. They concerned themselves with every aspect of road construction, although their most important concern was that roads should be built with a convex profile and with a surface of crushed small stones. John McAdam lived at Hoddesdon for a time, and his son was appointed Surveyor of many Hertfordshire turnpike trusts.

In 1827 the Postmaster-General appointed the famous engineer Thomas Telford to produce a survey and recommendations for a new Great North Road on the lines of the Holyhead Road. A Parliamentary Select Committee approved his plan, which would not only have greatly improved the carriageway itself, but would also have shortened the journey from London to Edinburgh by 20 miles. The fierce opposition from the towns and villages concerned (who might thus have obtained the by-passes they were to cry out for 100 years later) and the high cost of the project might not in themselves have prevented the scheme eventually coming to pass, had it not been for one event which occurred in the year the Great North Road Bill was drafted: the Rainhill Locomotive Trials of 1829.

125 *The* Black Horse, *Brent Pelham*

10

Law and Order

The mechanisms for the administration of justice and for keeping order grew without any clear specification of tasks or responsibilities. It was not by any means certain that the same offence, committed in the same place at the same time, would pass through the same channels, come before the same court, and receive the same punishment. As with public order, so with poverty. From time to time national legislation was passed, but the acts of Parliament were permissive, rather than compulsory, or else contained no specification for administrative machinery to put their clauses into operation. Thus, what actually happened depended on local enthusiasm.

Poverty and crime have always been thought of as being inextricably linked, even to the extent that establishments dealing with debt, poverty, vagrancy, and even lunacy, and those housing prisoners found guilty of some crime, were, if not actually the same, often contiguous and almost indistinguishable. The distinctions between poor houses, work houses and houses of correction were particularly difficult to grasp, and indeed, following the Workhouse Act of 1723, workhouses were set up which combined the functions of all three.

Prisons, as we think of them, are comparatively recent inventions. From early times, each village had its 'lockup' where those under suspicion could be held, and additionally there were the county's gaols, used to house those awaiting trial. The actual outcome of a trial, however, was not a prison sentence, but the administration of violence or humiliation. Until the 18th century the recorded outcome of trials at the assizes where more serious crimes were judged would be 'not guilty', 'guilty, whipped', or 'guilty, hanged'. There was a wide range of punishments for lesser crimes: periods locked in stocks or pillories, ducking on ducking stools, or judicial mutilation. As late as the end of the 18th century prison accounts include such entries as 'for burning William Gooke in the hand, 5s.' and 'for whipping Sarah Smith, 5s.'.

126 *Stocks at Brent Pelham*

Prison keepers provided their unwilling guests with only the bare minimum of comforts: those who had money could pay for such privileges as rooms to themselves, hot food and proper beds. The ordinary man was lucky to have a heap of smelly straw on the floor of a communal dormitory, and a basket of stale bread and odd scraps of food donated by local shopkeepers to share with his fellow prisoners.

127 *17th-century pargetting (decorative external plastering) in Fore Street, Hertford.*

In 1732 the gaol of Hertford was 'very grievously afflicted with an infectious distemper called gaol fever ... many prisoners have lost their lives and others have laboured under the same distemper to the danger of the health of the keepers of the gaol and others resorting to their assistance ...'. The keepers who made this protest cunningly emphasised the possible threat which the epidemic might pose to the authorities themselves:

> The distemper is of a very contagious nature and it may even be dangerous to your worships ... in our time a Lord Chief Baron, High Sheriff, two sergeants at law and several others received the infection in court and all perished of the same.

Nothing, however, was done, and in 1758 the inhabitants of the town again petitioned for some action, adding that there was now an outbreak of smallpox at the gaol. In 1759 a design was considered to remove the 'pestilential smell' from the prison by means of a ventilation system driven by a windmill on the roof. It was almost certainly not built.

Matters improved slightly for Hertfordshire prisoners when in 1775 an Act was passed permitting the construction of a new gaol and bridewell in Hertford. The gaol was built first, and in 1789 the keeper was able to report that debtors and felons were kept apart, that the cells were clean and well ventilated, although there was no separate accommodation for the sick, and no baths were provided. Further, inmates acquitted, or discharged for want of prosecution, were freed 'as soon as their irons could be got off, without fees'. The new bridewell was completed in 1792, and thereafter the justices preferred to use it as a central house of correction, rather than to make use of the smaller ones elsewhere.

By 1776, 48 parishes were provided with workhouses. Rules were strict, and every hour of the day was filled with work, a meal, or prayers, except for half an hour after lunch when children were permitted to play. Those who were ill were instructed to tell the workhouse master or mistress, 'who shall see all proper due attention paid which the disorder shall require and treat them with all humanity'. Those who refused to work were taken before a magistrate. Those objecting to or disobeying the rules were liable to a fine of 2d. in the shilling from their wages.

The original idea of the workhouse was that it should make use of the industrious poor in order to pay its own way, and this idea died hard. By the late 18th century, the poor were let to masters. Unfortunately, most of the inmates at this time were either very young, very old, or infirm. One solution to the problem of housing children was, apparently, to pay someone to take them away, as in this letter to the overseer of the Royston workhouse in 1796:

128 *Early Georgian house at Baldock*

> A considerable cotton manufacturer in this town [Warrington in Lancashire] having occasion for a number of boys and girls he hath so requested me to enquire from you the number that you have to put out, their ages, the sum that you will give with

each and whether besides you will be at the expense of their respective journies to Warrington ...

In some cases 'out-payments' were made to keep the paupers from coming into the workhouse at all.

Useful physical work was needed for the inmates of bridewells, and in Hertford in 1820 a recommendation was made that 'a mill for grinding and dressing corn is likely to be the most effectual mode of employing persons who are unwilling to work, and by the irksome fatigue of it, it is calculated to operate as a punishment and is less likely than other species of manufacture to interfere with the trades of honest inhabitants of the neighbourhood'. A treadmill was accordingly built and installed at Hertford; it could be worked by anything between 16 and 40 men. In 1827 it was reported that 'prisoners in the House of Correction have required additional food to enable them to work on the mill, and have shown debility from want of sufficient nourishment'. Despite this, in 1833 the justices discussed 'the propriety of increasing the speed of the mill with a view to rendering the punishment more severe'. A similar device was used at St Albans to pump water for the prison and part of the town.

The unrest associated with the long period of the French wars at the end of the 18th and the beginning of the 19th centuries, partly caused by the number of former soldiers roaming the land, and partly by a series of bad harvests, found local constables both inefficient and unwilling to deal with the protection of property. In the late 18th century, the well-to-do began to form Residents' Associations for their mutual protection. In the beginning these bodies, like the Great Berkhamsted and Northchurch Residents' Association, which was founded in 1794, simply collected subscriptions from their members and offered awards for convictions of felons. This idea was taken up by Stevenage and Hatfield in 1807, Rickmansworth in 1818 and about the same time by Hertford, Baldock and Watton.

The scheme was improved upon, however, by the association formed in Barnet, where the inhabitants employed their own police force in 1813. The policemen patrolled a wide rural area, and by 1836 consisted of one superintendent, eight sergeants and 80 constables. The Watching and Lighting Act, passed in the early years of the 19th century, enabled towns to form their own police forces: Hemel had one sergeant and two privates in 1837, and similar provisions were made at St Albans and Hertford.

In 1836 a Royal Commission was appointed to enquire into the best means of establishing a constabulary force. Crime was found to be particularly rife in rural areas:

> The depredations in some rural districts are carried on to such an extent as to threaten to put a stop to cultivation. This state of things is described in a communication from the Guardian at the Parish of Braughing: 'It is not an uncommon practice to lay open sheep folds and turn flocks loose at night ... and to lift gates off their hinges ... . During the whole of last winter scarcely a week passed without sheep, pigs, poultry, corn or straw being stolen, generally with impunity.

129 *Hertfordshire policeman in the 19th century*

Parliament passed the County Police Act in 1839. As it was an 'enabling act', that is, allowed counties to form their own forces rather than making it compulsory, the justices of Hertfordshire set up a sub-committee to enquire into the need for a new force in the county. They considered that the existing forces were effective. At St Albans, for example, it was reported that crime had dropped to 60 per cent of its previous level the year after the Borough Police Force was established. In the next year it dropped to 33 per cent of its original level. Generally, the towns were happy as they were, while the rural areas feared that their problems would be forgotten.

There were other objections, such as the surprisingly modern-sounding one from *The Reformer*, a Hertfordshire Whig newspaper, which expressed opposition because the new force would be under the control of the quarter sessions, rather than of a democratically-elected body. If the ratepayers paid the piper, *The Reformer* argued, they should also call the tune. The Rev. Newcomb of Shenley expressed darker fears with his suspicion that 'a rural police would be a very ready and willing instrument of tyranny and espionage—if bribed to it ... What little simplicity is left to the rustics would soon be destroyed by policemen'.

The sub-committee discovered, however, that the county was not even supplied with what traditional policing custom had demanded. Seven parishes contained no constable at all, and the reports made of the efficiency of some of those who were in office were revealing. Great Amwell reported 'none but old Dogberries' and Watford 'the usual leet old women'. In the event, the force which was set up in 1841 was smaller and slightly more expensive than the sub-committee had originally hoped, consisting of one chief constable, six inspectors and 60 constables, who cost £5,851 in the first year. Three-quarters of the cost of the county force was met from the rates until 1874, when the subvention from central government was increased to a half. The force was administered by the quarter sessions until 1888, after which the police committee consisted half of justices, and half of representatives of the new county council. The Police Act did not abolish the old parish constables, but took over their duties in respect of law enforcement, vagrancy and even weights and measures; the few remaining tasks were in practice shared out amongst members of the vestry. It was found necessary after a while to insist on basic literacy standards for members of the police, many of whom came from working-class families and tuition was provided.

Towards the end of the 19th century, communications and mobility began to improve. Telephones were installed in police stations in 1893, but not as part of the public system. Even as late as 1922, a private subscriber to the G.P.O., tired of running messages, requested that his local policemen should have a telephone installed. In the same year that the police gained telephones, bicycles were issued to them, and their riders were paid an additional 3d. per hour danger money. Six years later we read of a crack squad of police cyclists, the 'Scorchers', pursuing and halting speeding civilian bicycles! Speed traps for motorists (timed with a stopwatch) were set first in 1905, although the first Hertfordshire police car (a two cylinder, two-seater open tourer) was not purchased until 1913. Horses were still in service until 1928.

In 1833 the Poor Law Commission reported to Parliament on its findings. Generally, it believed that the existing system of workhouses and poor relief was not working, and that the conditions in workhouses should be rendered so obnoxious that people would seek out any employment rather than enter them.

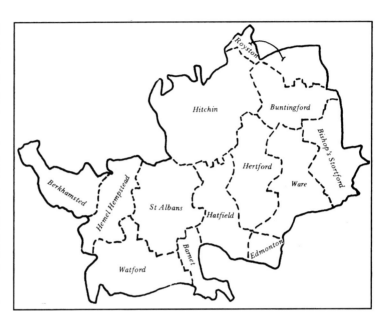

130 *The poor law unions of Hertfordshire*

The Act which followed divided counties into 'poor law unions'—Hertfordshire, for instance, into 12 of these areas—each of which had a large workhouse serving it. The poor were separated only by sex, regardless of whether they were paupers 'wilfully' through refusal to work, or from reasons of misfortune, age, infirmity or insanity. Every effort was made to make workhouse dwellers feel humiliated. Men had their hair shaved close to their heads, like convicts, and at Hitchin, in 1836, it was decided that

the dress of the paupers in the workhouse is not sufficiently distinguished from the dress of the labouring population of the neighbourhood, and consequently holds out a temptation to inmates to abscond with the clothing of the Union. Resolved that every item of clothing be stamped in a conspicuous manner with the letters H U in red paint, the coats with letters four inches in length, and the other parts of the dress with two inch letters.

By 1837 there were only three local bridewells still in use, at Berkhamsted, Hitchin and Buntingford. In 1843 the one at Buntingford was sold, but the building survives in Wyddial Road as Old Croft, a thatched private house, and the other two were converted into police stations.

Vagrancy continued to be a problem, as it had been throughout the ages. Irish immigrants tramping the county in search of work aggravated the situation, and after 1848 the poor-law unions provided casual wards for tramps, entirely separate from the main wards for the paupers. Tramps had to prove that they were able-bodied to qualify by doing physical work, by, for instance, breaking three hundredweight of stone for the roads. A bath was compulsory, but no other comforts were provided.

As in the old-style workhouses which they had replaced, the poor-law unions found no profitable or useful employment for the majority of

131 *In 1915 'St Albans prison, built in 1866-7 was finally closed. Its gateway became familiar to television viewers in the opening sequences of the popular series "Porridge".'*

their inmates. This was partly because it was those who had no choice in the matter who became the largest proportion of the workhouse inhabitants: the aged and chronically sick. In 1866 *The Lancet* attacked the Poor-Law Board for the inhumanity and illogicality of providing no medical treatment, and two years later the Board advised that 'sick wards should be better furnished'. In 1871 at Berkhamsted Union, however, the medical officer was required to provide all the paupers in the district with domiciliary care, but also to supply them at his own expense with medicine and bandages, the aim being to discourage him from 'pampering his patients with frequent visits or costly medicines'. The old feeling that the poor deserved to be punished for their misfortunes died hard.

In 1930 the operation of the Poor Law was transferred from the Unions to the County Council, which set up a Public Assistance Committee to operate the workhouses. The nature of these establishments had slowly altered, and with the advent of the Welfare State, several of them formed parts of hospitals, as at Shodrells, Watford, where the nurses' home is the old workhouse. Others became geriatric hospitals, as at Berkhamsted (demolished in 1967) and Ware (Western House). Buntingford became a hostel for the homeless in 1970. There was no prison in Hertfordshire after 1915, when the St Albans prison, built in 1866-7, was finally closed. Its gateway became familiar to television viewers when it was used in the opening sequences of the popular series 'Porridge'. Hertford Gaol was closed in 1879, two years after the control of prisons passed to central from local government hands.

11

The Coming of the Railways

The pattern of main-line railways in Hertfordshire is very similar to that of the turnpike roads, basically a radial one from the capital. However, whereas the turnpikes came into being largely as a result of the demands from the existing traffic, the railways were more speculative ventures which roused wild enthusiasm and fierce competition, as each group of would-be entrepreneurs strove to secure Parliamentary approval in the face of its rivals, who were promoting other routes. There was no national overall pattern, and no awareness of the possible long-term effects of the railway upon society. Like the road improvements, the Hertfordshire railways provided no coherent cross-county routes, running mainly south to north.

Although the preambles to bills put before Parliament in the hope of gaining permission for railways claimed that the shareholders were motivated by such considerations as 'providing additional and more expeditious Means of Communication with London and York and with the manufacturing Districts of Yorkshire and Lancashire' or 'enabling farmers and graziers to send fat cattle to Smithfield in a few hours', the real motivation was that of personal gain. Lord Salisbury showed great interest in the London to York scheme, and insisted that a station should be built close to his house at Hatfield. The Great North Road was moved further away from the mansion, at a cost of £8,000 to the railway company. When he was prime minister, Lord Salisbury had a saloon carriage and engine always under steam for his personal use. He also rearranged the schedules to enable his guests to make cross-country journeys by special trains.

132 *Weathervane at Bushey station*

The first railway through the county—the London and Birmingham Railway, which later became, as a result of mergers, the London and North Western Railway (L.&.N.W.R.)—followed the route of the Grand Junction Canal up the Tring Valley, and found itself with similar problems. At Tring, to keep to the ruling maximum gradient of 1:333, the engineers provided a cutting two-and-a-quarter miles long and 57 feet deep. The railway missed the town by two miles. At Watford, just like the canal builders, the engineers had to contend with the parks of Lords Essex and Clarendon. Unlike a canal, however, a railway cannot easily be turned into a landscape improvement, and a diversion was made involving a tunnel over a mile long, with an embankment 40 feet high south of it.

TRING CUTTING IN COURSE OF CONSTRUCTION. 1837.

133 *'The huge task of earthmoving was undertaken by navvies with horses, and was very dangerous.' The construction of the Tring cutting on the London and North Western Railway. Note the men with the wheelbarrows on the ramps. The barrows were attached to ropes over pulleys, and pulled by horses.*

At Tring, to keep to the ruling maximum gradient of 1:333, the engineers provided a cutting two-and-a-quarter miles long and 57 feet deep. The railway missed the town by two miles. The huge task of earthmoving was undertaken by navvies with wheelbarrows and horses, and was very dangerous. The Watford tunnel alone claimed ten lives, and in 1836-7, when the Tring cutting was being constructed, the West Hertfordshire Hospital had 43 admissions arising from accidents during the work, six of which were fatal.

The line was not completed to Birmingham until September 1838 because of difficulties with the Kilsby tunnel, but a horse-drawn coach service ran between Denbigh Hall and Rugby between April and the completion of the line.

Five branch lines were built to connect with the London and Birmingham main line. The Aylesbury one, opened in 1839, was the first branch line in the country. It had one station in Hertfordshire, at Marston Gate. The St Albans branch reached the gasworks (St Albans Abbey Station) in 1858. The Rickmansworth branch was conceived by Lord Ebury, who intended it to extend to Uxbridge. It was opened in 1862, and was worked by the London and Birmingham Railway for its private owners. A through service was provided from St Albans to Rickmansworth after 1871, until 1952 when this branch closed. The Watford loop and the branch to Croxley Green were added in 1912 and 1913.

Perhaps it is not surprising that the second main line in the county went up the Lea Valley, where the other navigable water route ran. The Northern Eastern Railway originally planned a route which went from London via Cambridge to Yarmouth, but Parliamentary sanction could not be obtained for the extension to Yarmouth, and funds did not even permit construction all the way to Cambridge. Broxbourne was reached in 1840, Harlow in 1841 and Bishops Stortford in 1842. The line to Hertford was opened in 1843.

134 *Engine on the Barnet line in the 1890s*

The 14-mile Buntingford branch was intended to be the Ware and Buntingford Railway, but opposition to the proposed route by landowners caused the junction to be re-sited at St Margaret's and the line to go to the east of Ware. The company began work in 1859, but had great financial problems, particularly since eight river crossings were involved. The line was finally opened in 1863, and carried passengers until 1964 and freight until 1965.

The 'Southbury Loop' via Theobalds Grove was an interesting project; it opened in 1891 with the intention of developing the residential area of Cheshunt and Edmonton. It did not succeed and closed in 1909, but in 1960 it was judged that demand at last made it viable, and it was re-opened.

By 1843 both the east and west of Hertfordshire were served by railways, but there was no development in the centre. Routes to York via Cambridge and Lincoln had been proposed and rejected in 1827 and 1835; the engineering problems of a railway line which would parallel the Great North Road were formidable. In 1844 two rival schemes were proposed by the Direct Northern Railway and the London and York Railway Companies. The two schemes and the two companies were combined in 1846 to form the Great Northern Railway (G.N.R.). Opposition from landowners—particularly that of Lord Dacre of Kimpton Hoo—prevented the new line going up the Mimram Valley. The decision to cross the valley to the east of Welwyn, threading between the parks of Lockleys and Tewin Water, led to the construction of the county's major industrial monument, the Digswell or Welwyn Viaduct, 1,560 feet long and nearly one hundred feet high, from which trains to the north plunge straight into a tunnel. The line was opened to Peterborough in 1850.

The Great Northern produced several branches, the first of which was the Hitchin and Royston line, in effect all that remained of the proposed Oxford and Cambridge railway. It reached Royston in 1850, and was extended to Shepreth in 1852, to join with the Eastern Counties line. The two (now defunct) branches which left the main line at the present site of Welwyn Garden City were originally conceived as a single cross-country route. The stretch from Hertford to Welwyn was opened in 1858. The line from Dunstable to Luton was completed in the same year, and reached Welwyn in 1860. The original intention was to cross the G.N.R., but the main line operators' objections proved insuperable. The temporary 'Welwyn' station located in uninhabited

135 *'Digswell, or Wel-wyn Viaduct, 1560 feet long and nearly 100 feet high.' Constructed to avoid the parks of the gentry in the Mimram valley, this viaduct ends in a tunnel.*

countryside was demolished and trains on both lines terminated at Hatfield.

A Hatfield-St Albans branch was completed in 1865 to be operated by the G.N.R., who bought it outright in 1883. It passed under the Midland line, and shared Abbey Station with the L. & N.W.R. A branch of the G.N.R. to Totternhoe, Whetstone and High Barnet was opened in 1872.

The pioneer underground railway, built as a 'cut-and-cover' project from Paddington to the City, opened in 1863 and was extended to Rickmansworth in 1887. The main line (Moor Park, Rickmansworth, Chorley Wood) was shared with the Great Central Railway after 1899. Plans for a route to Watford were halted by a refusal to give permission for an embankment at Cassiobury, and were not carried out until 1925. The Metropolitan line became part of the London Passenger Transport Board's system in 1933.

The railways destroyed the viability of the turnpike trusts, which were dissolved after 1862. Thereafter the upkeep of main roads was paid out of county funds and administered by a highways board, until ten years later control passed to the newly-created county council.

Although the railways permitted the rapid and relatively cheap transport of goods, the county as a whole remained predominantly agricultural during the 19th century. Towns which were fortunate enough to be served by railways tended to grow and develop light or agriculturally-based industries. New settlements came into existence near railways, causing a shift in the population of existing parishes, as occurred at Hemel Hempstead and Knebworth, and two-centred or straggling settlements as at Barnet, Potters Bar and Harpenden.

The junction between the branch lines to Dunstable and to Hertford from the Great Northern Railway was chosen as the site of the second garden city in 1926; it was probably because of the name the railway company had given the site (Welwyn Junction) that it was called Welwyn Garden City, when in fact it was between the parishes of Digswell and Hatfield.

136 *The railways and stations of Hertfordshire, with dates of opening and closing.*

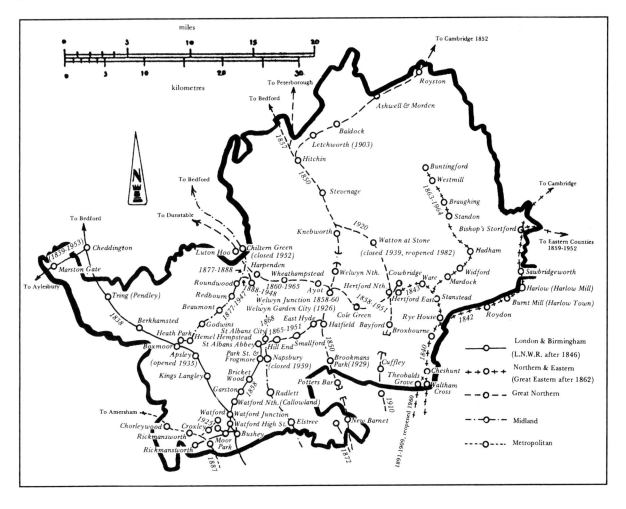

It was not, however, the increased mobility of goods which had the greatest effect on the county, but the increased mobility of people. In 1838, just after the opening of the London and Birmingham Railway, its official *Guide* stated that:

It [the railway system] has already begun to produce great material changes in society. Many who, but a few years since, scarcely penetrated beyond the county in which they were born are now induced to visit places more remote ... and to become acquainted with customs, manners and habits which previously were unknown to them.

Perhaps the greatest effect on the county was that the railways made it possible to work in London and live in Hertfordshire. The age of the commuter was about to dawn. Sydney Low summed it up in 1891:

The centre of population is shifting from the heart to the limbs. The life blood is pouring into the long arms of brick and mortar and cheap stucco that are feeling their way out to the Surrey moors, the Essex flats and the Hertfordshire copses ... the people of London will dwell in 'urban sanitary districts' straggling far down into the Home Counties.

137 *The* George and Dragon, *Codicote—probably the oldest inn in Hertfordshire*

12

Changes in the Countryside

Improvements to the roads through the turnpike trusts brought many changes to the county, and many small hamlets grew by a centripetal movement of people engaged in service trade, because the places were strategically placed as posting stations for stage coaches. Other significant changes resulted from the improvements in agriculture which were taking place all over England.

138 *Hertfordshire plough*

Hertfordshire produced a fine crop of writers on the subject in the 18th century. William Ellis dispensed gossip and farming lore from Church Farm, Great Gaddesden, and George Cooke of West End wrote *The Complete English Farmer* in 1750. Both D. Walker and Arthur Young produced useful surveys and summaries of the state of English agriculture, published respectively in 1795 and 1804.

'Melioration [improvement] of soils', enclosure and the rotation of crops by the inclusion of nitrogen-rich plants like turnips and clover, are the main messages of these authorities, and these practices brought new prosperity to farmers. The edition of Daniel Defoe's *Tour*, published in 1779, recorded the effects there of the new agricultural practices:

> A fruitful soil as it is managed; for it is certain, it is more indebted, for its fertility, to the sagacity and industry of the husbandman, than to nature ... . These cold and wet lands have been within these forty or fifty years greatly improved.

Walker described the field pattern in the county:

> The land is generally inclosed, though there are many small common fields, or lands, laying intermixed in small pieces, the property of different persons, which are cultivated nearly in the same way as inclosed lands; the larger common fields lie towards Cambridgeshire.

139 *Arthur Young*

Agricultural writers also urged the adoption of new machinery in farming, like seed drills, but it would appear from contemporary comments that this was only slowly adopted in Hertfordshire. Arthur Young commented in 1804 that he had 'passed through 100 miles of the County, enquiring for drilled crops, but neither seeing nor hearing of any'.

The mid-18th century was the golden age for Hertfordshire corn dealers, as corn prices rose rapidly. The county's closeness to London was eventually its undoing, as Londoners outbid the local market. Violence was never far below the surface as profitable scarcity became near-famine. In 1783 'incendiary fires' were reported, one at Potton

140 *Hornbeam*

causing many casualties and £25,000 worth of damage. Thirteen out-breaks of suspected arson occurred around Hitchin, where a letter was posted: 'You gentlemen, mealmen, bootchers and backers and Grocers of Hitchin ... if you don't sink we will burn you down as low as we cann'. Many similar threatening letters were received by gentry and corn-dealers over the next 50 years.

Some remarks made by Walker in his *Agricultural Survey* may be used to sum up the end of the 18th century:

> The scanty allowance of a parish to alleviate the wants of starving children, is a poor compensation to an honest hard-working father for the loss of that labour by which he had cheerfully sustained them ... . Provisions are dearer than in the metropolis, and much of the provisions with which the poor are fed are bought from thence, independent of groceries.

Agriculture remained the major source of employment for country people, although there were still, as there had always been, various small rural industries. Although the county possesses no great mineral wealth in the usual sense, quarrying and mining have taken place. The only noteworthy freestone is the hard chalk called Totternhoe Stone or clunch which crops out as a thin band on the north scarp face of the Chilterns. This was used as a building stone from at least the 12th century on-wards. It was exploited by adit mining, most notably at Ashwell and at Dunstable, just over the border in Bedfordshire. An unusual industry which was also important at Ashwell in the 19th century was the digging of phosphatic nodules and fossils, derived from the gault. These mis-named 'coprolites' were washed, crushed and treated with sulphuric acid to produce superphosphate fertiliser.

The fertile land between Hoddesdon and Wormley was used by market gardeners from early times, because of its easy transport to London. In the middle of the 19th century, commercial glasshouses came into operation here. Cucumbers and grapes appear to have been the first staple crops produced; tomatoes were not popular until later in the cen-tury. Flowers and foliage plants were cultivated as well. By the end of the century, the Lea Valley had about one-quarter of the acreage of glass for the entire country.

141 *A hurdlemaker*

At Hitchin there were lavender fields, and there was a distillery producing lavender water; other herbs were cultivated as well. Water-cress was a major Hertfordshire crop, and large hamper-like baskets of cress were a common sight on railway platforms. The history of the industry is not certain, but it is interesting to note that when Carl Linnaeus, the botanist, visited Hertfordshire in 1748, he made no mention of it although recording that wintercress (*barbarea*) was collected as a vege-table.

Forest industries continued to be important in the north-west, and to some extent, in the south of the county. Patten and clog makers, coopers and stavemakers, are all mentioned. Wooden shovels (needed for malting) and spoons were made. Beech and especially alder were suitable for bowls and other 'hollow wares'. William Ellis wrote about the alders and

the woodworkers who made use of them, in the watermeadows between Hemel and Watford, in the 18th century:

142 *'Large, hamper-like, baskets ... were a common sight on railway platforms.' The Bancroft osier beds at Hitchin.*

> The Berkhamsted and Cheshunt turners of hollow ware, who in this commodity make more consumption of this wood and Beech than in any other two towns in Great Britain ... with this wood ... make dishes, bowls and many other serviceable goods that are lighter and softer than the Beech or Elm, and they will bear turning thinner than most others ... and of this many of the frames of the matted and other chairs in London are made, as are pattens, clogs, and heels of shoes, gates, hurdles and small rafters.

Hurdle makers must have been necessary from early times, and sallow and willow were grown for this purpose along the Lea Valley south of Hertford. In 1825 the trees were cut on a nine- or ten-year rotation for hurdles. Basketmaking also uses willow; Wormley was a noted centre for this craft in the 16th and 17th centuries. It is a surprising fact that the bark of an oak tree was often comparable in value with the actual timber. This was because it was used by tanners. A mill grinding oak bark for this purpose existed at Hertford in the early 19th century.

143 *'Agriculture remained the major source of employment for county people.' The traditional garment was the Hertfordshire smock, seen here worn by Mr. Stevens of Tring in 1911, when he was 103 years old.*

French fashion influences meant that straw hats became very popular from the late 18th century, and 477,024 were imported in 1760 from Tuscany. With the cutting-off of continental supplies by the Napoleonic Wars, the English industry was given a boost. After about 1800, the process of splitting the straw was performed by either conical bone or metal 'cogs' attached to handles, or else by the Austin cutter, which had a pear- or bat-shaped wooden frame in which iron blades were fixed. Hitherto cottage industry had principally consisted of lacemaking, mainly confined to the north-west of the county around Berkhamsted and Tring.

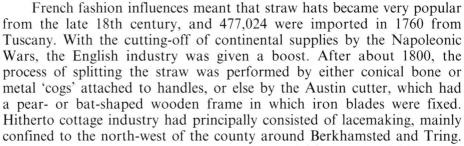

Straw plaiting was quickly popular throughout the county, earning the workers a very reasonable wage and giving them a new independence, much to the annoyance of local gentlemen and farmers, as Arthur Young noted:

> About Stevenage, spinning has given place to plaiting straw, by which they earn three or four times as much. The same is to be found at Hatfield; but Redburn is the place where the manufacture is most prevalent; where women will earn £1 1s. a week, and where a pound of straw is sold as high as 6d. After six weeks learning, a girl has earned 8s. a week; and some clever little girls even 15s. The farmers complain of it, as doing mischief, for it makes the poor saucy, and no servants can be procured, or any field work done, where this manufacture establishes itself.

At this time, an agricultural labourer could earn between 6s. and 12s. per week.

In 1861 the census records show that 8,598 women and 603 men were employed in the plaiting industry, although no doubt many more plaited part-time. In addition, 1,847 women and 147 men were makers of hats and bonnets. In some places the majority of the population seem to have been employed in the industry, as at Kensworth (then in Hertfordshire), where out of a total population of 891 persons, 151 women, 17 men

and 39 children were engaged in plaiting, and 39 women, 1 man and 5 children in hatmaking.

The lifestyle of straw plaiters was subjected to constant adverse criticism. Plait girls 'too often enter upon evil courses'; 'there is a great want of chastity among plait girls'. Young commented that, 'It is however, highly beneficial to the poor; a child can begin at four or five years old'.

Elementary schools for the poor, as distinct from the rather more pretentious grammar schools, had come into existence by the end of the 17th century, and by 1800 there were 29 endowed charity schools in the county. Sunday schools began in 1780 and gifts such as clothing were offered to ensure attendance. The religious societies aided the building of proper schools, and Wheathampstead school was built with a grant in 1815. Others followed, and enlightened squires made a significant contribution. The Abel Smiths at Watton built and maintained five parish schools, and the Giles Pullers at Ware had built one and helped to maintain three others by 1850. In 1853 these landlords were amongst the principal subscribers in the setting up of a teachers' training college at Hockerill, built by the religious societies but maintained by the state. It is significant

144 *'It is, however, highly beneficial to the poor: a child can begin at four or five years old.' The social importance of straw plaiting cannot be overestimated. The workers were female, independent, and more highly paid than male agricultural labourers, who formed the majority of the labour force. Straw plaiters at Charlton Mill, near Hitchin.*

145   *Austin straw splitter*

that the hereditary aristocracy, with the notable exception of the Cowpers, played very little part in the spread of education.

In many schools, straw plaiting was taught as a profitable incentive to attendance alongside the three Rs, but it is clear that in many instances all pretence of education was abandoned. Many so-called 'plait schools' were set up in the 19th century which were no more than children's sweatshops. The Factory Act of 1867 banned the employment of children under eight in handcrafts, and required those aged between eight and 13 to attend elementary school for at least ten hours per week. Education became compulsory in 1880, but truancy was rife until it became free 11 years later.

The decline of plaiting was swift, with the import of cheaper but in some ways superior straw twist from China and Japan. A writer in 1910 noted that he had recently bought 'a hank of twelve yards of coarse plait for one penny in Hitchin market'. At least one dealer was still buying English plait in 1922, and straw mats and boxes were still being made in the 1930s. Today, however, the industry has completely vanished.

We are fortunate in having two Hertfordshire diarists to give us their picture of life in the county in the first half of the 19th century. The first of them, John Carrington of Bramfield, was a small farmer in the early 1800s, who was already 71 when he began his record in 1797; he made his last entry in 1810. As well as being a farmer, he was also chief constable of his hundred, an Overseer of the Poor and surveyor of roads for his parish. Although we can be sure that he discharged his various duties conscientiously, his business meetings, usually held in local inns, were convivial occasions and almost always ended with a feast—one of the perks of the job:

> **15th March 1802**. To Wotton Turnpike Meeting at Crawley's *White Horse*. Paid 2-18-6 for Bramfield Parish ... Dinner Sr. Lyon Rost Beef fillett of Veal, Green Ham, Puding ...

146   *Wooden plait mill*

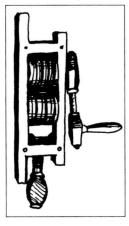

Among his many references to feasts and parties, Carrington often mentions benefit clubs, which he usually refers to as 'Drinking Clubs'. These were, in fact, the forerunners of the friendly societies which provided unemployment and sickness payments to their members and from which present-day insurance companies grew.

Carrington was in a sense retired, since the business of running his farm had been handed over to his son William, but he led a very active life with his various public duties. He is found undertaking the first census in 1801, noting 190 people in 28 houses at Bramfield. At Brewster Quarter Sessions he helped three widow licensees through their business, and then entertained them to dinner; periodically he would 'way the wts.,' since his duties as a constable included overseeing weights and measures.

The Napoleonic Wars brought him additional duties. In 1803 he noted that:

XIII *Welwyn Garden City*

XIV *Knebworth House from the herb garden*

XV *Letchworth, Wilbury Road*

XVI *Gazebos at Ware, mainly built with wealth derived from malt, overlooking the navigable waterway which took the product to London.*

This month we are Thretned to be invaded by one Boneparte, by the French, and England is to be divided amongst the French And every Man to be killed and the Women to be saved, So we are raiseing of men from 17 to 55 one Class and 15 to 60 the other Class, so Nothing but Soldiering three times a week.

In 1807 there was a 'great ballot from Men to serve King and Country'. Apart from volunteers, the forces of the crown were recruited by ballot –conscription by lottery, like the modern American 'draft'. Substitutes were accepted, however; Carrington's son William found a man willing to serve in his place for 20s. Sessions records show that of the 45,000 enlisted men from the county, 90 per cent were substitutes for those originally drawn by lot!

147   *John Izzard Pryor*

Our second diarist is John Pryor, who wrote his journal between 1827, when he was 53, and 1861. He was a step up the social ladder from Carrington; a middle-class brewer and country gentleman, holding the offices of deputy lieutenant and magistrate. He gives us some idea of the unrest of the early 1830s, when the agricultural labourers' frustration at their low wages, the high price of bread, the prevailing unemployment in the countryside and all the other restrictions imposed on them erupted in bouts of rick-burning. Pryor was concerned, however, not with ameliorating the causes of the problem, but with repressing the effects. 'Although Great rewards have been offered very few of the perpetrators of these diabolical deeds has yet been discovered. God grant that they may ere long!'

Hertfordshire seems, however, to have suffered less from the labourers' protests than other counties. Two factors in particular may have contributed to this. Enclosure—a major cause of grievance elsewhere— proceeded to a great extent in Hertfordshire by agreement, rather than by force. Alternative and remunerative rural employment was also available, in particular in the straw plaiting industry, and these sources of employment were unaffected by fluctuations in agricultural prices.

Pryor's diary gives a glimpse of the process of enclosure, and the problems it could involve. In 1840 he was involved in protracted negotiations at Sandon; the rights-holders were able to prevent the enclosure of the common, although agreement was reached over the enclosure of the former open fields. The Hertfordshire General Inclosure Act of 1845 eased the process, and about eleven thousand acres were enclosed during the next 30 years under the act. Large areas in the north-east of the county, however, continued to be farmed under the open-field system, including whole parishes such as Bygrave, Clothall and Wallington, right into the 20th century.

148   *John Bennet Lawes*

Pryor also mentions the use of manure: in 1828 he mentions men spreading saltpetre on the wheat, and in 1843 he was adding ammoniacal gas liquor to his compost. A note he made in 1844 is of particular interest for the history of agriculture:

I rode over to Standon. Finding my tenant R. Walby on the field, I looked over part of the farm with him ... R. Walby is Agent to Mr. Lawes for the sale of super phosphate of lime (a composition of bone dust and sulphuric acid etc. highly spoken of). I bought a bag weighing 2 cwt. by way of trial to drill in on 'Shoulder of Mutton Piece'.

'Mr. Lawes' was John Bennet Lawes, who inherited an estate at Rothamsted, near Harpenden, in 1834. In 1842 Lawes patented a process of making 'mineral superphosphate' by heating bone from spent animal charcoal with concentrated sulphuric acid. With the substantial income he gained thereby, the famous experimental work of Rothamsted began. Laboratories were built there in the 1850s, and Lawes himself was made a baronet in 1882 for his contribution to agriculture. In 1889 he founded the Rothamsted Trust, to which he conveyed the estate and £100,000. The work of the Trust continues today.

With the advent of the railways, droving ceased, and it became unnecessary to fold and fatten livestock within the county. The new practices brought about changes in the markets, as the Rev. J. Clutterbuck noted in 1864:

Of old markets, suffice it to say that there are 18 market towns in which the old system of selling wheat by the load of five bushels is still very generally followed ... . The modern practice of holding sales of fat stock by auction at such towns as Hitchin, Hertford, Bishops Stortford and Watford has assumed such large and increased proportions that it may be well to trace its development at the town of Hitchin. These sales, which were first held occasionally in 1852, took place in 1853 two or three times in a month, and ultimately in 1853 every week. A yard specially fitted up for the purpose was opened ... on 8th December, 1862.

Towards the end of the century the massive resources of the North American prairies undermined agricultural prices in Britain, and from the 1870s onwards agriculture entered a period of acute depression. Rents fell and farms remained empty as it became difficult for landlords to find tenants willing to take them on. However, a 50 per cent increase in the area of permanent pasture within the county took place; new farming practices to some extent compensated for the problems attending arable farming, and a new concentration on the growing of animal foodstuffs did much to counterbalance the fall in the demand for corn.

The introduction of a modern system of local government could only come after the extraordinarily complex maze of local boundaries in the county had been unscrambled. At Markyate, for instance, the administrative problems were acute. The town had grown up along the main road, and it was not a parish in its own right until 1888. The county boundary between Hertfordshire and Bedfordshire swept in from the fields, went along the main road, and then away down the middle of a side road. The effects of this are shown in a letter from the chief constable:

It would be convenient if a small portion of the Parish of Flamstead were transferred from the County of Hertford to the County of Bedford so that the whole of the village of Markyate Street should be in the County of Bedford. The north west part of the main street of the village being in the hamlet of Humbershoe, County of Bedfordshire, the south west part of the same street being in the Parish of Flamstead, County of

Hertford, and the east side of the street being in the Parish of Caddington, County of Hertfordshire and the whole being in Markyate Street ... .

The village of Coleshill was wholly surrounded by Buckinghamshire. Royston, which, it will be remembered, was a creation of the local priory, lay within five parishes until 1540, and was divided between Hertfordshire and Cambridgeshire until 1897.

149 *Boundaries ancient and modern. The ancient ecclesiastical parishes and the civil parishes compared.*

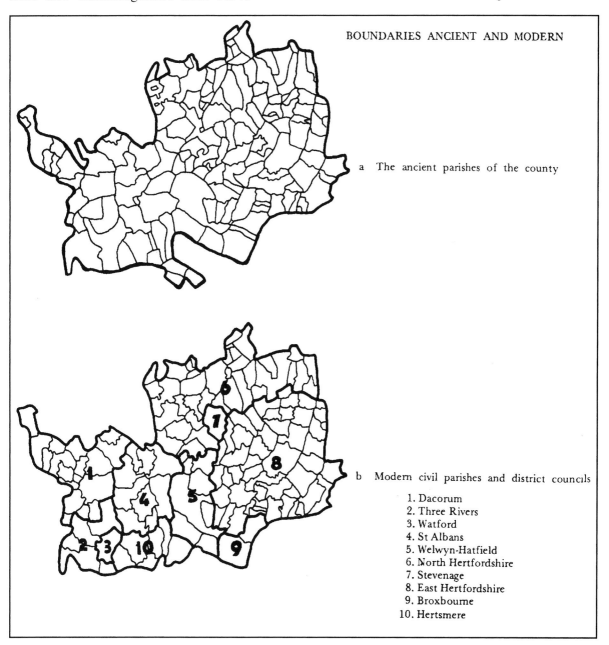

BOUNDARIES ANCIENT AND MODERN

a   The ancient parishes of the county

b   Modern civil parishes and district councils

1. Dacorum
2. Three Rivers
3. Watford
4. St Albans
5. Welwyn-Hatfield
6. North Hertfordshire
7. Stevenage
8. East Hertfordshire
9. Broxbourne
10. Hertsmere

These anomalies made it impossible on occasion for the most conscientious local officials to perform their duties, like John Petell, who wrote on 4 September 1824 that

> the justices request me to make a return of Property [in] the Hamlet of St Thomas Chapel which is out of my power to do, As the Counties of Hertford and Bedford are so intermixed with one another that no one knows how to divide them, The Hamlet of St Thos Chapel has always paid one third of the Ickleford County Rate, and has always been paid out of the Poor Book of the Parish of Meppershall as it is impossible to ascertain one county from the other ...

Most of the difficulties with Hertfordshire boundaries were along the northern edge, and were dealt with by measures between 1888 and 1906. No further changes were deemed necessary until the creation of the Greater London Council in 1965, when Barnet, Totteridge, Arkley and Monken Hadley were transferred to London. Potters Bar was transferred to Hertfordshire at the same time; it had previously been in Middlesex, which then ceased to exist as an administrative county.

If one considered ecclesiastical boundaries, the situation was no less confusing. Prior to 1845, 22 parishes were administered by the Archdeaconry of St Albans in the diocese of London; 77 were in the Archdeaconry of Huntingdon in the diocese of Lincoln; three were peculiars of the Dean and Chapter of St Paul's, and six came under the Commissary and Consistory Courts of the Bishops of London. In 1845, by some perverse logic, the situation was tidied up by placing the whole county in the diocese of Rochester, Kent. In 1877 the diocese of St Albans was formed, and the whole county then came under its jurisdiction (see map, p.115).

At the beginning of the 19th century, the civil parish—that is, the area for which a separate Poor Law rate was made—was almost always coterminous with the ecclesiastical parish. There were, of course, anomalies; hamlets rated separately from their parishes, detached parts of parishes and even 'extraparochial' places. At Hitchin, part of the market was in the parish of Tewin and the *Cock Hotel* was in Shillington! Acts of 1857 and 1868 dealt with extraparochial places, either abolishing them or else making them into proper parishes. At the same time, the ecclesiastical parish ceased to be an instrument of local government, as compulsory church rates were abolished. Acts between 1876 and 1882 provided for the absorption of detached portions into surrounding parishes.

The Local Government Act of 1888, which created the county council and set up the administrative county, allowed further alterations to be made to civil parishes by local government. A further act of 1892 permitted areas with a population in excess of two hundred to elect parish councils.

13

Urban Life and Change

Politics

In 1704 Daniel Defoe wrote of Hertfordshire:

> The County is under several characters. The part of it adjoining to Bedfordshire is Whiggish and full of Dissenters. That part adjoining to Huntingdonshire, Cambridgeshire, and Essex, entirely Church, and of the High Sort. The gentlemen of the Royston Club settle all the affairs of the county and carry all before them, though they behave with something more modesty, or at least carry it closer, than former days. Mr. Freeman is master of this part of the county as to parties.

Prior to the Reform Act of 1832, Hertfordshire returned six members: two for each of the boroughs (St Albans and Hertford) and two for the county. The wining and dining of electors and the control of candidates by patronage had already become established in the 17th century. In 1654 Sir John Wittenwronge's election expenses included 175 gallons of sack, 165 gallons of French wine, 1,044 gallons of beer and perhaps not surprisingly, 'loss of pewter and lynen'. Mr. Freeman, referred to by Defoe, was elected in 1690. At first Sir Charles Caesar had been returned, but this was overturned on appeal:

> Resolved that Quakers, having freehold, and refusing to take the oath when tendered by the Sheriff, are incapable of giving their votes for Knights of the Shire for that reason ... . That Ralph Freeman is duly elected a Knight of the Shire for this County.

Elections during the 18th and early 19th centuries were so corrupt that petitions against their results were frequently made, usually securing the reversal of the original decision. It is recorded that electoral bribes were not usually paid at St Albans until 28 days after the election—the maximum period allowed for the submission of an appeal.

The political situation at the end of the 18th century was described unemotionally by Thomas Oldfield in 1794, with a frank acceptance of things as they were. Of Hertford he wrote, 'Baron Dimsdale possesses the principal interest in the Borough, and can secure the election of one member. The other is generally contested'. The borough of St Albans was notorious for its corruption, and was eventually disenfranchised in 1852. Oldfield wrote of it 60 years before:

150 *Holywell House, residence of the Marlboroughs*

> The influence in this Borough is divided between Earl Spencer and Lord Grimston, each of whom returns one member to Parliament. These two noblemen have long contended for superiority, but neither of them has an interest sufficient to obtain a majority over the other.

151 *'A great lady went thither.' The Marlborough almshouses at St Albans, built in 1736, are said to have been designed by Sarah, Duchess of Marlborough.*

The Grimston connection with St Albans began in 1652, when Sir Harbottle Grimston, a member of Parliament and Master of the Rolls, bought Gorhambury and married into the Bacon family. The Spencer interest derives from the manor of Holywell and the long influence exerted in the district by the Jennings family, whose most famous member was Sarah, Duchess of Marlborough. In her day she took the patronage of one parliamentary seat for the borough upon herself, although not always successfully. In 1705 a contemporary noted that Mr. Gape 'has carried it at St Albans, notwithstanding a great lady went thither to oppose him'.

152 *Sarah Churchill, Duchess of Marlborough*

Of the county, Oldfield wrote that it had 'the singular advantage of maintaining its independence, which it has neglected no opportunity of exerting ... an attempt was made at the last election to introduce Mr. Hale to the representation of the County under the patronage of the Marquess of Salisbury and Lord Viscount Grimston, but with very little success'. The independent nature of the voters manifested itself on many occasions, as for instance in 1736, when Mr. Caesar was arrested for debt and imprisoned at the dissolution of Parliament, whereupon 'the independent freeholders repaired to Hertford in bodies, and at their own expense, proposed Mr. Caesar, and elected him by a great majority. He was restored to liberty and the service of his affectionate constituents'. The reason for the independence of the county is simple: there were few old families in the county at large with inherited interests. Most of the numerous landowners were self-made men with fortunes derived from business or banking.

The Reform Act of 1832 gave the county three seats, and left the borough representation unchanged. However, as we have seen, St Albans was disenfranchised for corruption in 1852; in the 20 years since the Reform Act, more than £37,000 had been spent on elections, of which £24,600 had gone on bribery, an average of £3,000 per election. The population of the borough was about 7,000, of which about 500 persons had the vote; each vote cost about six pounds. In 1867 the Representation of the People Act reduced Hertford's parliamentary representation to one member. It was totally disenfranchised by the Redistribution Act of 1885, which divided the county into two divisions, each electing one member.

Towns, Trade and Industry

The historian Simpson wrote in 1746:

> As there is little or no manufacture in the Shire, which is full of Maltsters, Millers, Dealers in Corn, etc., the Trade would be inconsiderable, was it not for its being every Way a great Thorough-Fare, and for its neighbourhood to London, which makes the Chief Market-Towns to be much frequented for the sale of Wheat and Barley, and all sorts of Grain, not only the growth of this, but of several other Shires.

An excellent example of the combined effects of industry and social mobility is supplied by Watford, which was described by Defoe in 1724 as 'a genteel market town, very long, having but one street', a description which was repeated almost verbatim by directories and guides for the

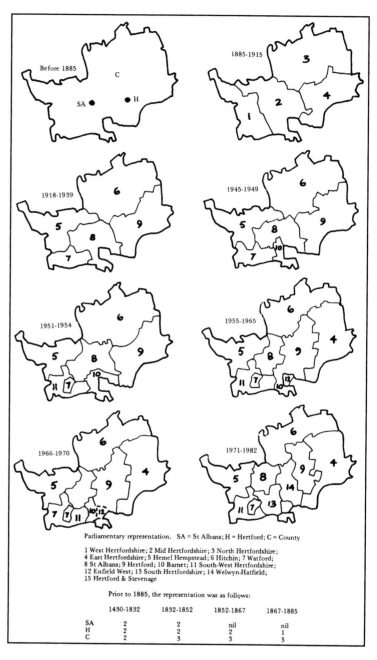

Parliamentary representation. SA = St Albans; H = Hertford; C = County

1 West Hertfordshire; 2 Mid Hertfordshire; 3 North Hertfordshire; 4 East Hertfordshire; 5 Hemel Hempstead; 6 Hitchin; 7 Watford; 8 St Albans; 9 Hertford; 10 Barnet; 11 South-West Hertfordshire; 12 Enfield West; 13 South Hertfordshire; 14 Welwyn-Hatfield; 15 Hertford & Stevenage

Prior to 1885, the representation was as follows:

	1430-1832	1832-1852	1852-1867	1867-1885
SA	2	2	nil	nil
H	2	2	2	1
C	2	3	3	3

153 *Parliamentary representation, pre-1885 to 1982*

154 *Milestone on the Grand Junction Canal*

next 100 years. The Grand Junction Canal opened in 1801, and the railway in 1837. The population rose during the first half of the 19th century at a rate which was just above the average for the county. There were two paper mills, one silk mill, and one flour mill. Between 1861 and 1900 the population rose by three and a half times its 1861 level, whilst that of the county as a whole rose by less than a half. The description of the town in the *Victoria County History of Hertfordshire*, written at the beginning of this century, is most revealing.

There are houses of the smaller description [which] have attracted a large number of workers engaged in London, while the comparative cheapness of the land, and the good railway facilities, have resulted in the erection of a number of factories and works ... The residential portion ... lies to the north of the town. It is well-timbered and contains many pleasant residences with large gardens and grounds, mostly occupied by gentlemen engaged in business in London.

'Business gentlemen' were encouraged to make their homes at Watford by the gift of free first-class railway passes, valid for 21 years, which were provided with each of the 'pleasant residences'.

The malt industry continued to grow throughout the 18th century, when 5,000 quarters (1,250 tons) of malt were sent by barge to London from Ware every week. In the 19th century there were 70 malthouses in Ware alone. The early history of Hertfordshire banking is closely connected with malting and brewing: Lucas of Hitchin, and Christie and Cathrow of Hoddesdon were banker-brewers. Many of the London brewers chose to make their homes in the county, naturally, on the eastern border.

The manufacture of textiles continued on a small scale throughout the 17th and 18th centuries in Hertfordshire. In the 19th century there were silk weaving mills at Rickmansworth and Tring, the latter employing 500 people. At the same time, about a hundred other persons at Tring were working at the much harsher task of weaving canvas on hand looms.

Papermaking, which had begun so early in Hertfordshire (see Chapter 7 above), seems to have died out until the 17th century. In 1649 Sopwell Mill at St Albans was referred to as a paper mill, although it had reverted to flour milling by 1691. Hatfield Mill made paper in 1672, and continued to do so until 1835. Standon Mill made paper in 1713, but by 1835 was a sawmill. In the 18th century, there were at least eighteen paper mills in the county, mostly along the Chess, Colne and Bulbourne rivers on the western side of the county.

In 1798 a Frenchman invented a process for making continuous paper on an endless web of wire mesh. Henry and Sealy Fourdrinier bought an interest in the English patents, and developed the machinery in this country owing to the troubled state of affairs in France. The machine first worked at Frogmore Mill on the Gade in 1804, and was the prototype for most modern ones, although the Fourdriniers were ruined by the costs of research and development. Meanwhile John Dickinson of Nash Mills made paper successfully on a cylindrical mesh,

155 *Mid-Georgian mill at Frogmore*

and patented the process in 1809 while the Foudrinier process was still imperfect. Dickinson's principle is still in use for the manufacture of millboard and composite papers, and was used for the manufacture of cannon cartridges in the Peninsular War and at Waterloo.

156 *'Rather resembling a village than a manufactory.' The Apsley Mill paper works at Hemel Hempstead.*

The Foudriniers were bankrupt by 1810, and Dickinson built up the paper industry almost without a rival. By 1888 the company had mills at Apsley, Nash, Kings Langley, and Croxley, and had leases on Two Waters, Frogmore, and Batchworth. The company's central premises at Apsley Mill were described in 1819 as 'rather resembling a village than a manufactory' and cover 30 acres today.

In the 19th century urban expansion was taking place at a pace too fast for the existing facilities of the towns, intended for a smaller population, to be able to cope. Overcrowding led to the spread of disease, which bred easily in open sewers and in mounds of rubbish deposited in the streets. At Hitchin, for example, 850 cases of typhus were recorded in 1848, of which 162 proved fatal. A report on the

157 *Victorian pump and lamp at Hemel Hempstead*

epidemic condemned the use of open sewers, and the frequent contamination of wells, as well as the fearful overcrowding. There were only 59 toilets in the town, which had a population of 7,000 (including nearly a thousand paupers). Hitchin was the second town in England to set up a Board of Health, in the same year. John Pryor recorded the reaction of his local vestry to the provisions of the Public Health Act, passed by Parliament in 1848:

> November 6, 1848
> I attended a Vestry soon after eleven this morning to consider putting into force the sanitary measures recommended by the Government and sent down to the Guardians of the Parishes throughout the kingdom for warding off much as possible an attack of cholera ... We made a list of names for a committee of inspection.

> November 13, 1848
> The persons appointed last week, having already taken a cursory view, were ... directed to make a general inspection ... a week was to be given for the removal of general nuisances and a fortnight for the erection of privies.

The Chartist Experiment at Heronsgate

1846 saw the beginning of an extraordinary urban experiment in Hertfordshire which foreshadowed the development of 'garden cities' in the county by almost a century. It was undertaken by Feargus O'Connor, a leading member of the National Charter Association. The Chartist Movement had developed in reaction to the harsh economic conditions which prevailed in the early decades of the 19th century, and sought to improve the conditions of working people through the provision of an extension of the franchise and other electoral reforms. O'Connor hoped to create a new kind of social structure in which the dominance of great landowners would be replaced by an egalitarian system, with many small landholders leading an idealised 'medieval' life. In 1846 he bought 103 acres of land at Heronsgate or Herringsgate near Chorley Wood, for £2,344.

After the coppices which covered it had been cleared, the land was divided into small plots: 13 of four acres, five of three acres, and 17 of two acres. Each was provided with a substantial cottage with outbuildings for livestock. There was a school, but no church or public house. Finance was provided by private subscriptions to the Chartist (later the National) Land Company, initially priced at £1 6s., and plot allocation was made by lottery amongst the 70,000 subscribers, the size of the holding being dependent upon the number of shares held. Those with two shares, for instance, would, if successful in the lottery, receive a two-acre plot and £15 to help with the cost of seed and stock; four shares gave four acres and the sum of £20. The Company continued to own the land, and the rents, after paying off the cost of the land, would go towards purchasing further acreages. O'Connor believed that in this way he would house 24,000 families in the first five years.

A Parliamentary Select Committee was set up to examine the scheme, and the evidence of one witness summarised their conclusions:

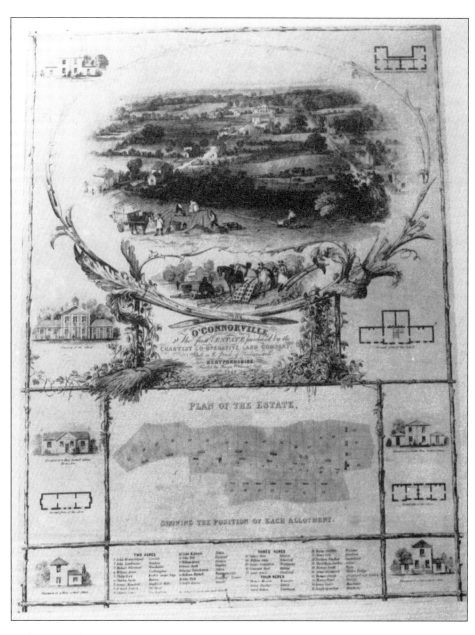

158 *'An extraordinary urban experiment in Hertfordshire.' The advertisement for Feargus O' Connor's Heronsgate, showing land allocation and house designs.*

The plan of buying farms and dividing them into three or four acre allotments, to be cultivated by the spade by artisans and weavers from the manufacturing towns, is about as hopeful as would be a scheme for buying large power-loom factories, pulling down the steam machinery, and appropriating each of the looms to be worked by a farm labourer.

This belief proved correct, and very soon it became apparent that the tenants could not earn enough to pay their rents. In any case, the committee decided, the scheme was illegal, since it constituted a lottery for

159 *Bulwer Lytton*

gain. Further, the Company had not been established on a legal basis, and did not constitute a friendly society. Proper accounts had not been kept. However, it must be added that there was no intention to defraud: in his enthusiasm, O'Connor was subsidising the scheme from his own pocket. Perhaps because the committee felt the plan was doomed to failure, and also because of O'Connor's great public popularity, it decided to take no action, merely stating that it should be left 'to the parties concerned to propose to Parliament any new measures for the purpose of carrying out the expectations and objects of the Company'.

In 1851 the Company was declared bankrupt, and was closed by an act of Parliament. The estate was taken over by the Court of Chancery and eventually sold off in lots to private owners. The well-built cottages for O'Connor's working families still exist, now much-prized dwellings in Metroland. Feargus O'Connor, who had tried to keep the scheme afloat by every possible exertion, even milking the cows himself, was placed in restraint after a scene in the House of Commons in 1852 and was thereafter kept as a lunatic until his death from epilepsy in 1854.

Famous Residents in Hertfordshire

Throughout the 19th century, as throughout history, Hertfordshire was the home of many famous people, amongst whom politicians form a significant group. Edward Bulwer (1803-73) was first elected to Parliament for Lincoln in 1831, and represented St Ives from 1832-41, during which period he wrote several plays and popular novels, including *The Last Days of Pompeii*. He became a baronet in 1838, and inherited the Knebworth estate in 1843, after which he added his mother's maiden name of Lytton to his own, as she had requested in her will. In 1852 he became a M.P. for Hertfordshire, and held the seat until he became the 1st Baron Lytton in 1866. He is best remembered as a writer today; he published over twenty novels and plays. His reputation amongst his contemporaries was as an outstanding all-rounder, and he was a member of a literary circle which included Dickens and Wilkie Collins.

160 *William Lamb*

William Lamb (1779-1848) was first elected to Parliament in 1805. His wife, the poet and novelist Lady Caroline Lamb, is remembered today principally for her tragic infatuation with Lord Byron. In 1827 Lamb became the Secretary for Ireland and three years later, on inheriting the title of Lord Melbourne, entered the House of Lords, where he held the post of Home Secretary. Following the collapse of Lord Grey's government in 1835 over the Irish Question, Lord Melbourne became Prime Minister, which he remained with only a brief interval until 1841. In 1842 he suffered a paralytic stroke and retired from politics, and died at Brocket Hall, his family seat. He was first minister, and a personal mentor, to the young Queen Victoria after her accession in 1837.

Melbourne's Foreign Secretary was his brother-in-law Lord Palmerston (1784-1865), who inherited Brocket Hall through his wife in

1848. He had entered Parliament in 1807, and was Secretary for War from 1809 to 1828. He was also well known for his humorous writings and poetry. In 1830 he became Foreign Secretary, and exerted a powerful influence on the conduct of foreign affairs, whether in or out of office, for the next 20 years. In 1852 he became Home Secretary, and in 1855, at the age of 70, Prime Minister. From then on until his death in 1865 he was without a doubt the dominant figure at Westminster. No measure that he disapproved of could pass through Parliament, and no government could stand without him. Even the monarch submitted to his prejudices, although she wrote privately, 'I *never* liked him, or could ever in the least respect him'.

Lord Robert Cecil (1830-1903) was a direct descendant of Lord Burghley, Elizabeth I's leading minister, and in his turn became Prime Minister to Queen Victoria. He first entered Parliament in 1853, and was an outstanding member of the Commons until he succeeded to his title (becoming the 3rd Marquess of Salisbury) in 1868. He was Foreign

161 *The home of two Prime Ministers of England, William Lamb (Lord Melbourne) and Lord Palmerston — Brocket Hall, Lemsford.*

162 *Palmerston*

163 *The 3rd Marquess of Salisbury*

164 *'Lord Robert Cecil was a direct descendant of Queen Elizabeth's leading minister and in turn became Prime Minister to Queen Victoria.' As 3rd Marquess of Salisbury, in effigy he greets visitors at the gates to Hatfield House.*

Minister from 1878 to 1880, and Prime Minister 1885-6, 1886-92 and 1895-1902, holding the office for longer than any other. In his day, Hatfield House saw the lavish entertainment of royalty, diplomats, the rich and the famous.

14

The Last Hundred Years

In 1898 Ebenezer Howard, a self taught stenographer and son of a baker-confectioner from the East End of London, published a book called *Tomorrow A Peaceful Path to Real Reform*. His intention was to suggest an alternative way of living, combing the best features of both town and country life:

I will undertake ... to show how ... equal, nay, better opportunities of social intercourse may be enjoyed than are enjoyed in any crowded city, while yet the beauties of nature may encompass and enfold each dweller therein; how higher wages are compatible with reduced rents or rates; how abundant opportunities for employment and bright prospects of advancement may be secured for all; how capital may be attracted and wealth created; how the most admirable sanitary conditions may be ensured; how beautiful homes and gardens may be seen on every hand; how bounds of freedom may be widened, and yet the best results of concert and cooperation gathered in a happy people.

In 1899 a 'Garden City Association' was established, with the object of putting Howard's visions into practice. The book was revised and republished in 1902 under the title *Garden Cities of Tomorrow*, and at the same time the Garden City Pioneer Company was founded with a share capital of £20,000.

Howard's Garden City, based partly on the concept of the model industrial village, such as New Lanark, differed from it and from Bournville and Port Sunlight in that it:

endeavoured to obtain as many different trades as possible because, obviously, a town dependent on one large factory, or on one particular

165 *'A self-taught stenographer and son of a baker-confectioner.' Ebenezer Howard, father of the Garden City Movement in his later years.*

166 *Bookplate— Garden Cities of To-morrow*

167 *Early 19th-century yeoman*

class of trade, is very hard hit, if such a factory or trade is suffering from a trade recession.

After a number of possible sites had been considered, the first Garden City Company was incorporated in 1903 with a share capital of £300,000. The new company purchased 3,822 acres of mainly agricultural land in the parishes of Letchworth, Willian and Norton. The total population of these parishes in 1901 was 566. The population of Letchworth Garden City was about 10,000 by the outbreak of the First World War.

The very beginning of the century had seen the men of Hertfordshire on active service abroad and both the Volunteers and the Yeomanry fought in the Boer War in 1900. In the First World War the Hertfordshire Regiment served on the Western Front throughout the hostilities, whilst squadrons of the Yeomanry were in Egypt, Gallipoli, Mesopotamia and Syria, as well as at the Somme. The new Artillery, formed in 1908, were sent to France in 1915, but were then re-embarked for Egypt, where they joined the Yeomanry in the pursuit of the enemy through Syria.

Aerial warfare came early to the county; in fact, the first airmen killed in action died in a crash at Willian during army manoeuvres in September 1912. During the Great War, London Colney provided the Royal Flying Corps with an airfield which was the temporary home of several flying aces. German airships came over the county, and a number of bombs were dropped. A Zeppelin raid on Hertford in October 1915 was very destructive of life and property, but airships proved vulnerable to aircraft armed with incendiary bullets. The first Zeppelin shot down on English soil fell at Cuffley in September 1916, and another airship was destroyed at Potters Bar a month later.

The architects who turned Howard's dream into reality created neither the cosy community of a village, nor the impressive confidence of a town. There is no excitement or majesty, but it worked, and its influence was seminal. The spacious park-like layout, adequate gardens and cottage-style dwellings became the inspiration of countless inter-war suburbs. Lionel Munby, in his book *The History of Hertfordshire Landscape*, puts his finger on the problem of writing about Letchworth:

> The most striking thing about Letchworth is that there is nothing striking to see. The difficulty ... is that so many things that were done for the first time have become commonplace since.

On 30 May 1919 Ebenezer Howard bought at auction 1,458 acres of the Panshanger estate for £51,000. The site was 20 miles north of London, and was to become Welwyn Garden City. In October a further 694 acres were purchased from the Salisbury estate, and on 20 April 1920 Welwyn Garden City Ltd. was formed. The first house was occupied just before Christmas of that year.

Despite Letchworth's distance from London and the fact that it was not on the main railway line, by 1926 there were 70 factories employing some 4,000 work-people. At Welwyn Garden City, however, housing

preceded industry, and the initial development was therefore to a great extent that of a dormitory town, parodied by a famous Punch cartoon of commuters in gumboots. The factory area was eventually laid out, however, with mains services, sidings from the railway, and a road connection to the Great North road. The first major industrial development was the construction of the impressive Welgar (from Welwyn Garden City) Shredded Wheat factory in 1925. The population had risen to about fifteen thousand at the outbreak of the Second World War.

The Hertfordshire Yeomanry were in the throes of a reorganisation to form Hertfordshire regiments of field artillery at this time. No. 79 trained for anti-aircraft work; the regiment served at Le Havre in 1940, and then defended Swansea and Neath before moving to Algeria in 1941. From here they eventually took part in the Italian campaign. 135 Regiment were sent to Malaya, and were captured by the Japanese at the fall of Singapore shortly afterwards. 86 Regiment were the first guns to land on the shores of France on D-Day, and 191 Regiment landed three days later.

The 1st Battalion of the Hertfordshire regiment garrisoned Gibraltar from 1943-4 and then served in Italy and Palestine. The 2nd Battalion trained for combined operations and, after helping to establish a bridgehead at Ver-sur-Mer on D-Day, were dispersed to reinforce the advancing Allied army.

168 *The first major industrial development was the impressive Welgar ... Shredded Wheat factory.' Ploughing in Welwyn Garden City about 1930, with the industrial development in the background. The silos and chimneys of the Shredded Wheat Factory are in the top right-hand corner.*

169 *'Successive abbots were largely responsible for the destruction of Verulamium.' Cricketers play today over the buried ruins of the Roman town, part of the walls of which can be seen on the right. Behind them are the abbey, built mainly of Roman tiles quarried from Roman buildings in the Saxon and Norman period, and the 14th-century abbey gateway.*

De Havilland Aircraft were manufactured at Hatfield, where the Mosquito was designed. At Leavesden the Mosquito was made by de Havilland and the Halifax bomber was manufactured by London Transport. Handley Page had a works at Colney Street. Between the wars De Havilland had established a training field at Panshanger near Welwyn, and many R.A.F. pilots were trained here. Hunsdon was an important operational field, from which 85 Squadron flew during the Battle of Britain. It was later famous for its 'pinpoint men', trained to tackle special bombing targets, and the raid which breached Amiens jail, releasing many imprisoned Resistance members, was flown from Hunsdon. No. 2 Army Co-operation Squadron had Lysanders at Sawbridgeworth, aircraft almost synonymous with cloak-and-dagger operations. The Special Operations Executive (and perhaps other secret organisations) were at Brickendonbury and The Frythe, Welwyn. The latter, known as 'Station Nine', produced and tested a miniature submarine, amongst many other secret weapons.

Heavy bombers flew from Hertfordshire: these were American Flying Fortresses, based at Nuthampstead. Bovingdon Airfield had just been constructed for the R.A.F. when the U.S.A. entered the war; the station was lent to the U.S.A.F. as a training station, and Bushey Hall served as the U.S. Fighter H.Q.

Hertfordshire escaped the worst of the Blitz. It lacked major conurbations and the heavy manufacturing industries, and was not on a flying route to London or any other major target. Only about four thousand high explosive bombs fell in the county, and some towns, notably Ware, remained almost unscathed. The later 'doodle-bugs' and rockets were targeted on the metropolis, and their flight paths were not intentionally directed over Hertfordshire. Only 107 of the nine thousand odd V1s and 47 out of 1,115 V2s fell in the county.

Between the World Wars, central government made little contribution to solving the problem of city growth. A Royal Commission set up
to consider the problems did not cease during hostilities. The Abercrombie
or Greater London report was published in 1944, and went so far as to
suggest ten possible sites for new satellite towns to relieve the pressure
on London. The labour government of 1945 created a new Towns Committee which acted with astonishing speed. The New Town Act was
passed in 1946, and Stevenage was the first place to be designated a
New Town, on 11 October 1946. Hemel was the second, on 4 February
1947, and Hatfield and Welwyn Garden City followed in May 1948.
The New Towns were created by 'quangos' called Commissions for the
New Towns, with the extensive powers necessary for their work, including that of compulsory purchase.

At Stevenage and Hemel Hempstead the planners attempted to form
the New Towns by creating small 'villages' or 'neighbourhood communities', each with its own churches, shops and schools, and at Hemel,
where the topography naturally divides the site, this idea seems to work.
At Stevenage, however, from the visitor's point of view there is a bewildering sense of similarity between the neighbourhoods.

The Second World War accelerated the process of industrialisation
foreshadowed by Letchworth. More people came to live and work in the
county; businesses evacuated into the county saw the attraction of staying there permanently. In the 19th century the main cause of immigration into Hertfordshire was the transport revolution: but it was not long
before industrialists appreciated the advantages of moving into larger
and cheaper premises close to the potential labour force which this population movement had created. Today the traditional Hertfordshire
industries—malting, brewing, milling—have declined to the point of
extinction; there are no commercial mills, and the last major maltsters

170 *'At last Hertfordshire had a valuable
mineral resource – gravel,
mainly in the Vale of St
Albans.' Gravel extrac-
tion is an industry which
has a major impact on
the landscape. This
extraction plant is at
Beech Farm, close to the
site of Hatfield airfield.*

171 *Stevenage new
church*

closed in 1995. In recent years proximity to the capital and the excellent transport links, coupled with the pleasing environment, have attracted 'sunrise' industries—electronics, telecommunications and computers—as well as major financial and insurance companies.

Modern Portland cement became available in 1900 and made reinforced concrete viable. At last Hertfordshire had a valuable mineral resource—gravel, mainly in the Vale of St Albans—the valley of the protoThames. The deposits are shallow and are removed by an open-cast quarrying. The industry has an impact on the landscape quite disproportionate to the numbers it employs. About three hundred people are engaged in quarries covering 200 acres, mainly in the Vale of St Albans, and the Lea and Colne valleys. Until recent years the land was left derelict after it had been quarried, but nowadays great efforts are made to ameliorate the destruction. Dry pits provide valuable tips for rubbish and can then be reinstated for arable use. Most of the pits, however, are in river valleys, and can thus become permanent lakes, which are now valued as nature reserves and sites for water sports. One of the attractions of the currant scheme to extract gravel from Panshanger is that it will eventually provide a country park after careful restoration work. Before industry obtained the use of the land it had been landscaped by capability Brown and Repton!

About one-tenth of all the aircraft workers in the country worked in Hertfordshire in the 1960s. The establishment of the De Havilland Aircraft Company in Hertfordshire was a typical example of the advent of industry to the county. The company had a flying club in open unspoilt country a mile or so from Hatfield. The creation of the Barnet by-pass in 1928 effectively put the site beside the Great North Road, and the Company then moved their works there from Edgware, to exploit labour from St Albans and Welwyn Garden City. Between 1930 and 1939 the numbers employed rose from 900 to 4,820.

172 Ancient and modern. This picture shows a British Aerospace 146, one of the last aircraft to be developed at Hatfield, over Stanborough, between Welwyn Garden City and Hatfield. Three routes of the Great North Road can be seen below it. To the right can be seen the original route via Lemsford, from which the New Road (Macadam, 1805) diverges. This in turn is cut by the new A1 motorway. The lakes are not flooded gravel pits; they were deliberately created as a recreational area by the local council.

At Hatfield Britain's first supersonic plane, the DH110, was developed. From this came the worlds first jet airliner, the Comet.

When in 1992, largely as a result of the cold war, British Aerospace decided to close the Hatfield works, dire effects were predicted, particularly for local employment. The local council stated that 2,300 people would lose their jobs, as one in eighteen of the local labour force was employed there, and that £15m of goods and services were purchased from Hertfordshire companies. In the event, the local unemployment

figures for the succeeding years were slightly better than the county average.

The reasons for this are complex, but two are of particular historic note. One is that the work force is now far more mobile than any time in the past; the other is that the nature and style of the employment has changed dramatically. In 1971, manufacturing accounted for 43 per cent of the labour force and services for 51 per cent; in 1981 the corresponding figures were 33 per cent and 60 per cent; by 1995, 26 per cent and 69 per cent. During the same period there had actually been a nett decrease in full-time employment in the service industries. Many 'hi-tech' industries have replaced the old 'metal-bashing' manufacturing. An astonishing statistic is that about 40 per cent of the workforce in the County are university graduates or have equivalent qualifications, although 16 per cent have no qualification at all.

The national 'bulge' in the birthrate after the Second World War was exaggerated by the sudden influx of young people with families into the New Towns, with the result that in 1953 the increase in the Hertfordshire school population was 6,000 a year, equal to the total number of pupils in a large town. A collaboration between John Newson, Director of Education, and the architect Johnson-Marshall produced a remarkable burst of school building; 148 new primary schools and 40 secondary school were constructed in the next twenty years. The bulge has passed through the system, and at least twenty schools have been decommissioned since 1971; in many cases the site has been sold for development.

The 1944 Education Act required the County to submit schemes for technical and further education. Three major colleges were planned: at Letchworth, Watford and Hatfield. Alan Butler, a director of the de Havilland Aircraft Company, gave 90 acres of his own land at Roe Green, close to the A1, on which a technical college and secondary school were built. The college opened in 1952. In addition to the courses at a low level, predominantly in engineering and building, de Havilland transferred their technical college to the site and seconded their staff, and more academic courses in Aeronautics were included. In 1952 HNC, diploma and extramural London degree courses were being taught, and in 1969 the college became a Polytechnic. In 1992 it became the University of Hertfordshire.

John East selected Elstree as an ideal place for location photography in 1914, as it was beyond the range of London's haze and fogs. Studios were later built, and films have been made at Elstree and Boreham Wood by A.B.C., M.G.M., and E.M.I., as well as by Associated Television. The site is listed for statutory protection. Eighty films were made at Welwyn Garden City between 1932 and 1942. One notable recent production at Boreham Wood was 'Star Wars', a film which broke all box office records, and netted £88 million in the first four years after its release in 1977. The studios are now used by the BBC.

Leavesden Airfield, which had seen the development and manufacture of jet engines from the famous Goblin to the Rolls Royce RB211 used on Tristar, ceased to be a factory in 1994, with the loss of 3,600 jobs. It has found a new lease of life as a film studio. The James Bond movie 'Goldeneye' was made there and a TV film 'Peggy Su' is in production. Three 'prequels' of 'Star Wars' and a Sci-Fi film 'Mortal Kombat Annihilation' are planned. Other films are made on derelict sites, almost on an *ad hoc* basis.

The great mobility of labour already mentioned, which was not foreseen by the planners of the New Towns, is largely possible because of the motor car. Only much larger counties, Essex and Kent, have more cars. In Hertfordshire 10 per cent of families do not own a car. 35 per cent have two cars, compared with the national figure of 24 per cent. There are more miles of road in the county than in comparable Bedfordshire, and yet a significantly higher number of cars per unit lengh of road.

In the 1920s a movement began to keep traffic from towns by means of by-passes. One of the first Hertfordshire ones opened in 1928, and was recorded admiringly by *The Observer*:

> Only country-lovers of the most myopic tendencies will fail to rejoice at the opening of the by-pass that carries the Great North Road by Welwyn instead of through it. For the truth is that these by-pass roads, unlovely though some of them are (remember they have hardly had time to grow beautiful) are doing excellent work in the preservation of rural England.

Since then a bewildering number of by-passes, 'traffic schemes' and 'circulatory systems' have appeared, with varying, and not always happy, effects on the quality of life. The latest 'improvements' are 'traffic calming measures' which include noisy rumble strips, jarring speed humps, slaloms, unsightly 'gates' at the beginning of villages, unexpected traffic islands and mini roundabouts, as well as hideous coloured strips down rural roads.

In 1924 the author Hilaire Belloc, not usually associated with visions of the future, suggested that there should be 'motorways' to separate users of the internal combustion engine from other road users. He cited as an example a route from London to Birmingham. Thirty-five years later the M1 was built through Hertfordshire almost exactly as Belloc had envisaged. The county now includes a long section of the M25 and part of the A1 has been upgraded as motorway from the M25 to north of Baldock, at Radwell, where lay the Slough of Despond which motivated the first turnpike in the 17th century.

One tacit assumption of the Garden City movement, at the beginning of the 20th century, was that the raw materials and the energy required could be brought to the workplace and the products could be distributed to the customer. This proved to be all too true, as elsewhere in Britain, where the roads are filled with massive trucks carrying often trivial objects. In retail distribution twenty years ago the attractions of the larger town centres were threatening the survival of the shops in the smaller ones, most of which have succumbed. Today it is the growth of easily accessible out-of-town superstores and 'retail parks' which is threatening the survival of the town centres. Shopping is being made into a recreation. Perhaps the weekly visit to the superstore should be looked upon as the modern equivalent of the medieval weekly visit to the market.

At the beginning of the century 83 per cent of the county was agricultural land and about 20,000 men were engaged in agriculture. Most of the work on the land was done by muscle power—either that of men or of horses. Most industry was connected with the traditional occupations such as milling, the nationally important malting, and brewing. 64 per cent of the land is still agricultural but only about 5,000 men are involved, most of them operating or driving machines—1 per cent of the labour force is earning a living from 64 per cent of the land. At the same time there is only one brewery, McMullens of Hertfordshire and there are no commercial mills or maltings.

Before the First World War, the *Victoria County History* said:

> The industrial position of Hertfordshire is probably ... stronger than ever before. The absence of coal or mineral wealth renders it unlikely that any exceptional development can be looked for, but the prospects of a lower wage bill and the provision of cheap electric power may do much to attract manufacturers from the great towns.

This century has seen so many changes that it would be foolish to predict so glibly what might happen in the next.

173 *'The county now includes a long section of the M25 and part of the A1 has been upgraded as motorway from the M25 to north of Baldock, at Radwell, where lay the Slough of Despond which motivated the first turnpike in the 17th century.'*

Sources

During the writing of this book I have consulted a wide spectrum of original sources, from scrappy memoranda, through unpublished manuscripts to official records. Printed sources, too, have ranged from impressively-bound limited editions to flimsy newspapers. Often the flimsiest and scrappiest survival, the very one that might be thought the most ephemeral, has proved the most rewarding. For example, the problems relating to county and parish boundaries were illuminated by a memorandum about the Markyate police (p.115), which chanced to be in the county archives, and the fate of the workhouses (p.100), as with many events this century, could only be discovered from newspaper reports.

To anyone wishing to discover more about a particular place or subject, the obvious starting point is a library index. The local studies library index at County Hall can lead you to printed books, photocopies of parts of books, pamphlets, magazines, and to carefully-preserved back numbers of newspapers. Almost all the material for the last chapter was found here. In the same building one can consult official records in the County Record Office. The staff of both establishments are friendly, sympathetic and helpful.

Books
The following are outstanding as containing extensive bibliographies:
Johnson, W. Branch, *Local History in Hertfordshire*, 1964
Robinson, G., *Barracuda Guide to County History Volume III, Hertfordshire*, 1978
Thwaite, M.F., *Periodicals and Transactions relating to Hertfordshire*, 1959

Adams, B.D., *Verulamium Museum Catalogue of Anglo Saxon Antiquities*, 1971
Addison, Sir W., *The Old Roads of England*, 1980
Albert, W., *The Turnpike System in England*, 1972
Ashby, M., *Stevenage Past*, 1995
Barton, P. and others, *The Peasants Revolt in Hertfordshire*, 1981
Bede, trans. Garmonsway, *Ecclesiastical History of the English Nation*
Bedfordshire Archaeological Journal
Bowden, R.A., *Genealogical Sources (Record Office)*, Revised edition 1981

Bonser, K.G., *The Drovers*, 1976

Branigan, K., *Town and Country*, 1973

Catt, J.A., *Quarternary History of the Hertfordshire Area*, 1978

Chauncy, Sir H., *The Historical Antiquities of Hertfordshire*

Clutterbuck, R., *History of the County of Hertford*, 1815-27

Cockham, F.G., *The Railways of Hertfordshire*, Second edition 1983

Crofts, J., *Packhorse Waggon & Post*, 1967

Curtis, G., *A Chronicle of Small Beer*, 1970

Cussans, J.E., *History of Hertfordshire 1870-1* (reprinted 1972)

Darby, H.C. and Campbell, E., *The Domesday Geography of South-East England*, 1962

Davis, K.R., *Britons and Saxons, The Chiltern Region 400-700 A.D.*, 1982

de Soissons, M., *Welwyn Garden City*, 1988

Defoe, D., *Tour Through the Whole Island of Great Britain* 1724 (and later edns.)

Dony, J.G., *A History of the Straw Hat Industry*, 1942

Drury, G.H., *The Face of the Earth*, 1959

Ellis, W., *Practical Farming* or *The Hertfordshire Husbandman*, 1732

Evans, H., *New Towns, The British Experience*, 1972

Evans, J., *The Endless Webb*, 1955

Faulkner, A.H., *The Grand Union Canal*, in Hertfordshire, Second edition 1993

Field, R., *Hitchin: A Pictorial History*, 1991

Filler, R., *A History of Welwyn Garden City*, 1989

Gardner, H.W., *A Survey of the Agriculture of Hertfordshire*, 1967

Glendinning, V., *Hertfordshire*, 1989

Gough, J.W., *Sir Hugh Middleton*, 1964

Hadfield, C., *Canals of the East Midlands*, 1966

Hertfordshire Archaeology

Hertfordshire Countryside

Hertfordshire Past & Present

Hertfordshire's Past

Hertfordshire Topic

Johnson, W.B., *The Industrial Archaeology of Hertfordshire*, 1970

Johnson, W.B., *Hertfordshire*, 1970

Johnson, W.B., *Memorandoms For ... The Carrington Diary*, 1973

Jones-Baker, D., *The Folklore of Hertfordshire*, 1977

Jones-Baker, D., *Old Hertfordshire Calendar*, 1974

Kingston, A., *Hertfordshire During the Great Civil War*, 1894

Le Hardy, W. (ed.), *Guide to the Hertfordshire Record Office*, 1961

Matthias, P., *The Brewing Industry of England 1700-1830*, 1939

McWhirr, A., *Verulamium*, 1971

Miller, M., *Letchworth: The First Garden City*, 1993

Morris, J. (ed.), *Domesday Book: Hertfordshire*, 1976

Moss-Eccardt, J., *Ebenezer Howard*, 1974

Niblett, R., *Roman Hertfordshire*, 1995

Osborn, N., *A History of the Hertfordshire Police*, 1969

Page, W. (ed.), *The Victoria County History: Hertfordshire*, 1906-14

Pahl, R.E., *Urbs in Rure*, 1965

Pevsner, N., *The Buildings of England: Hertfordshire*, Second edition 1977

Purdom, C.B., *The Building of the Satellite Towns*, 1949

Renn, D., *Medieval Castles in Hertfordshire*, 1971

Robert, R., *Historic Hertfordshire*, 1968

Rodwell, W. et al., *Small Towns in Roman Britain*, 1975

Rolt, L.T.C., *The Inland Waterways of England*, 1950

Rook, T., *Before the Railway Came - Welwyn 1820-1850*, 1994

Rook, T., *County Maps and Histories - Hertfordshire*, 1989

Rook, T., *Hertfordshire Histories - Roads*, 1991

Rook, T., *Hertfordshire Histories - Welwyn a Simple History*, 1995

Rook, T., *Of Local Interest - A Book of Welwyn Pubs*, 1986

Rook, T., *Welwyn Beginning*, 1968

Shirley, D. (ed.), *Hertfordshire: A Guide to the Countryside*, 1978

Smith, T.P., *The Anglo-Saxon Churches of Hertfordshire*, 1973

Swinson, A., *The Quest for Alban*, 1971

Taylor, P. and Corden, J., *Barnet, Edgware, Hadley and Totteridge: A Pictorial History*, 1994

Thomasson, A. J. and Avery, B.W., *Soil Survey 3*, 1970

Toms, E., *The Story of St Albans*, 1975

Transactions of the East Hertfordshire Archaeological Society

Transactions of the St Albans Architectural & Archaeological Society

Urwick, W., *Nonconformity in Hertfordshire*, 1884

Wacher, J., *The Civitas Capitals of Roman Britain*, 1966

Walker, D., *A General View of the Agriculture of Hertfordshire*, 1785

Ward, D., *Digswell from Domesday to Garden City*, reprinted 1995

Wheeler, R.E.M. and T.V., *Verulamium*, 1936

Wigens, S., *Famous Authors in Hertfordshire*, 1970

Webster, N.W., *The Great North Road*, 1974

Young, A., *A General View of Agriculture in Hertfordshire*, 1804 (reprinted 1971)

Index

References to the colour plates are given in **bold**